22

CHINA

CHINA AT FO

CHINA
AT
FORTY
Mid-Life Crisis?

Edited by
DAVID S. G. GOODMAN
and
GERALD SEGAL

CLARENDON PRESS · OXFORD
1989

Oxford University Press, Walton Street, Oxford OX2 6DP

Oxford New York Toronto
Delhi Bombay Calcutta Madras Karachi
Petaling Jaya Singapore Hong Kong Tokyo
Nairobi Dar es Salaam Cape Town
Melbourne Auckland

and associated companies in
Berlin Ibadan

Oxford is a trade mark of Oxford University Press

Published in the United States
by Oxford University Press, New York

British Library Cataloguing in Publication Data
China at forty: mid-life crisis?

1. China. Political events, 1949–
I. Goodman, David S. G. 1948– II. Segal, Gerald,
1953-
951.05
ISBN 0–19–827354–1

Library of Congress Cataloging in Publication Data
China at forty: mid-life crisis? / edited by David S. G. Goodman and
Gerald Segal.
Includes index.
I. China—Political and government—1976–
I. Goodman, David S. G. II. Segal, Gerald, 1953–.
DS779.26.C47345 1989   320.951—dc20   89–8615
ISBN 0–19–827354–1

Set by Page Bros (Norwich) Ltd

Printed in Great Britain by
Courier International Ltd.
Tiptree, Essex

PREFACE

As this book passes from proof to publication, China is indeed in crisis. We cannot claim to have predicted the events of May–June 1989, but we are proud to have been close to the 'spirit of Beijing'. As is evident from the subtitle of *China at Forty*, we understood China to be heading for a major crisis.

We chose not to update the book, in part because China is clearly now in for a period of uncertainty and adjustment. But we also felt that the analysis of the present crisis still stands, for it explains its roots without getting too lost in the fascinating, if bloody, details of recent events.

It is important to keep in mind that the recent unrest did not spring suddenly from the specific demands of student demonstrators in the spring of 1989. The political and economic reforms that we highlight have deep-rooted problems that can be traced back to the major changes of the past few years. It was already clear at the time this book was sent to the publishers that something had to change in China, and even now we do not know what the new changes will look like.

We have been pessimistic about the fate of the reforms. In the short term, the searing experience of the Beijing massacre will only exacerbate the underlying tensions. By the time this book is published, in time for the October anniversary, at best the picture will be only somewhat clearer. At worst, China may be slipping back towards Cultural Revolution-style politics with extreme attacks on opponents. In all but name the reforms might be over, both in politics and economics.

In the immediate aftermath of the shooting in Beijing, such pessimism is prominent in most analyses. But a more realistic hope would be that because the Party and Army remained more united through this crisis than most observers thought, then the repercussions will also be less intense. It is certainly clear that any serious political reform will not be on the agenda, but some optimism can be expressed about economic reform.

It is a central theme of this book that reform is essential for China. Nothing in politics is inevitable, but it is hard to imagine that China can turn its back on at least parts of the economic reform agenda. While the people of China have shown in the past that they are willing to do without political reform, they are far more insistent on the need to see improvements in their economic well-being. An incorrigible optimist might even go so far as to suggest that a tougher political leadership might even be better placed to force through tough economic decisions about price reform and greater liberalization of the market.

But with so much that is uncertain about Chinese politics, not to mention the disturbing uncertainty about whether Deng Xiaoping will remain alive or in charge by the time China's fortieth year is out, it is fruitless to speculate about scenarios. In the chapters that follow, we have identified the key problems and lines of reform that are necessary if China is to move forward. Sadly, it remains true that China is in crisis—only even more so.

15 June 1989

Gerald Segal

CONTENTS

ABBREVIATIONS

CCP   Chinese Communist Party
CPPCC   Chinese People's Political Consultative Conference
DP   Democratic parties.[the non-conformist parties]
GDP   Gross domestic product
GNP   Gross national product
KMT   The Nationalist Party [Kuomintang, or *Guomindang*: the ruling party in the Republic of China]
NIC   Newly Industrialized Country
NPC   National People's Congress
PRC   People's Republic of China
ROC   Republic of China
RMB   *renminbi* [People's currency]
SEZ   Special economic zone

NOTES ON CONTRIBUTORS

Marc Blecher is in the Department of Government, Oberlin College, Ohio.

Max Boisot is Director of the China–EEC Management Programme, Commission for Restructuring the Economic System, Beijing.

Terrell Carver is in the Department of Politics, University of Bristol.

Anita Chan is an Associate at the Contemporary China Centre, the Australian National University.

Harlan W. Jencks is a Research Fellow at the Center for Chinese Studies, University of California.

Li Jun is a Research Fellow at Wolfson College, Oxford.

Michèle Ledíc researches China's foreign trade and energy at Birkbeck College, University of London.

Lawrence R. Sullivan is a visiting Associate Professor of Political Science, Center for Chinese Studies, University of Michigan.

Lee Lai To is Senior Lecturer in the Department of Political Science, National University of Singapore.

INTRODUCTION

GERALD SEGAL

Is China at forty having a mid-life crisis? If crisis is understood in its Chinese sense of danger and opportunity, then China is in crisis. This is not to suggest that either the country is about to disintegrate or that Communist rule is about to collapse. But it is a crisis in the sense that the rulers recognize that the policies of the past are insufficient to cope with the major challenges of the future, and they are not agreed on what needs to be done as a result. This is as much a crisis of confidence.

But crisis is a word that seems to come easily to the lips of China-watchers at the end of each decade. In 1959 there was the failure of the 'Great Leap Forward', in 1969 there was the chaos of the 'Cultural Revolution' and in 1979 there was the uncertainty of the radical reforms. Of course, crisis sells copy. Nonetheless, many of the crises have been real and dire.

Of course, not all people are intimidated by their fortieth birthday and China, as China, has been around for millennia. But 1 October 1949 marked a major break with the Chinese past in that the country had a Communist revolution. Therefore, to be more specific, we are assessing forty years of Communism in China. But Communism has to be assessed with a clear sense of its Chinese characteristics. China did not have the first Communist revolution, but it was the largest—affecting the quarter of mankind that then lived in China. Given the lengthy traditions and great civilization that developed in pre-revolutionary China, the Communist revolution could not be expected to eliminate all previous traditions.

So how are we to judge forty years of Communism in China?[1] While there are some objective measures, such as growth in GDP or educational performance, most revolutions are not (at least initially) about such standards. They are more concerned with changing people's minds and habits. What is more, the world outside will judge the revolution by its own, sometimes different, standards of relative success. Thus, we are left with two, sometimes different standards of measurement—the one from inside and the other from outside. Both can be compared by looking at the major elements of revolution.

Rather than dwell on the past, contributors were asked to focus on the challenges. But writing in 1988, aware that the thorny nettle of price reform had been avoided rather than grasped, the contributors have all tried to look beyond the immediate headlines. This is a time for reflection, especially when China is trying to reform while allowing often incompatible systems and ideas to coexist. Most chapters capture the essential dilemma for a 40-year-old China—reform is essential, but reform will challenge the ruling system and its guiding Party, perhaps leading to restraint on reform. Nowhere is this challenge to authority set out more sharply than in the issue of economic reform.

Economic Prosperity

Of course China is a richer country after forty years of Communist rule. But economists will admit that measuring prosperity is subject to great uncertainty. Currency fluctuation, a black economy and regional diversity are only some of the more obvious reasons for caution in using statistics to answer the question of how much richer China has become.

China's own leaders admit that the country could have been far richer than it now is because previous policies were often seriously misguided. The tragedy of the 'Great Leap Forward' is perhaps the most obvious example of economic disaster because of what can only be described as 'lunatic' policies. The best estimates suggest up to 30 million Chinese died as a result of the related famine—a death toll far in excess of anything seen in the post-war world. What is worse, barely five years later, in the mid-1960s, Chinese leaders again lurched into economic insanity with the 'Great Proletarian Cultural Revolution'. The revolutionary motives might have made some sense—the idea that the revolutionary spirit should not be lost—but the practical impact on a society that needed to get beyond the revolutionary stage, was disastrous.

Only with the death of Mao Zedong in 1976 did China begin a sustained campaign to regain lost time and prosperity. The decade of reform since late 1978 has shown some of the most dramatic growth rates of any country. Until late 1988, when major problems were confronted because of the failure to implement serious price reform, China could claim that it was well on its way to making up for lost time. As it contemplates its 40th anniversary, the sense of optimism has dimmed.

The recent pessimism is in part derived from that other necessary aspect of the reform programme, the opening to the outside world. Greater contact made more Chinese aware of what success was achieved by foreigners, even those nearby. Although the original motive for Chinese reform stemmed from the failure of the domestic system to produce the goods it promised, it was also stimulated from the outside world when China recognized just what others had done while China experimented with revolutionary models.

By making use of some of the admittedly unreliable economic statistics, the comparison to the outside world is less than encouraging. In 1965, the Indian GDP was 70 per cent the size of China's. By 1986 the non-Communist Indians had gained 5 per cent on China. Canadian and Indian GDPs in 1965 were roughly the same, but by 1986 China's GDP was only 83 per cent the size of that of Canada. Of course, China's average growth rate between 1965 and 1980 was 6.4 per cent, but since 1980 it has been a staggering 10.5 per cent—the highest in the world over the same period. But the World Bank still listed China's per capita GNP as roughly $300, nearly the same as India and 4 per cent of that of Hong Kong.[2] It is true that some of China's neighbours had done every bit as poorly over the same period, most notably Vietnam and Indonesia. But Taiwan, South Korea, and Malaysia, not to mention Japan and the developed Pacific world, had increased the gap very sharply with China.

This game of comparison can be played out in far greater detail than is possible here. Further details can be added about the growth in specific sectors, and most notably the ability to feed most Chinese because of sharp increases in cereal production. But the central point remains—China has done well, but could have done much better. Because of policy fluctuations and the stop-start pattern of growth, many opportunities were lost. Even in the 1980s' age of reform, as one acute observer noted, there have been 'more swings than roundabouts', and even the swings seriously damaged economic growth.[3]

It can be argued that so long as there is growth, the verdict on China at forty must be positive.[4] But as the recent crunch in the reform programme suggests, not all growth is good, especially when it is uneven. Waste becomes massive and some of the disastrous features as seen in the 'Great Leap Forward', can ensue. In periods of high growth, high expectations are raised, inequalities are often exacerbated and political unrest cannot be very far behind. Hence another often-cited image to describe the risky modern Chinese reforms—riding a racing tiger.

Intellectual and Social Affairs

Judging success in the far more subjective realms of intellectual and social affairs is next to impossible. The revolution in 1949 was made by Communists and one's view of the necessity to restructure people's thoughts reflects one's judgement about the goals of Communism. It is true that China was never a liberal democracy as understood in the West and much of the greater willingness by the West to excuse China's policy on human rights stems from an appreciation of China's special past.

By the less culturally-forgiving criteria of Amnesty International, China has not done well and remains one of the most restrictive societies. The unflattering contrast with the Soviet Union in the age of reform shows China to have slipped further behind in terms of what is loosely called political reform. Despite the symbolic existence of a multi-party system in China, even socialist pluralism is far from a reality.

In fact, it is hard to argue that there has been any progress (to reveal a western bias) towards greater pluralism. Yet there have been many roundabouts in policy as leadership policies shifted. Intellectuals have known the exhilaration of the 'One Hundred Flowers' or 'Democracy Wall' periods. But they have also known many anti-rightist campaigns and the more recent attempts to quash what was called 'spiritual pollution'. Students are still a potent force in politics, as seen in the 'Cultural Revolution' or the purge of Hu Yaobang in 1987. Yet in both cases the students were best seen as tools of factional politics among the leaders rather than a manifestation of political pluralism and legal dissent. Indeed, it is the absence of a legal framework as understood in the West, and the reliance on moral precepts, that marks out the approach to intellectuals and pluralism. As John Fairbank regularly reminds us, dynastic despotism well pre-dates the coming of Communism to China.[5]

The usual riposte of Communist rulers (at least until Gorbachev), was that group rights always take precedence over those of the individual. Although Chinese minorities, especially in Tibet, would not accept that even this group-oriented approach to rights has been satisfied, it is true that the general welfare of the people has improved. It is hard to recall the chaos that was China forty years ago. The depth of drug addiction, poverty, malnutrition, and illiteracy, to name but a few, was legendary. That China is no longer known for any of these failings, much as Africa now often is, is a testament to the revolution.

Of course, the Chinese still admit how far they have to go. In the field of education, China has only recently made it a major priority, especially at the higher levels. China may have more college and university teachers than India and Brazil, but in 1987 the total number of students was the same as in the much smaller Brazil. India had twice as many students despite a smaller population. Only 2 per cent of college-aged young people in China are enrolled in higher education, compared with 9 per cent in India, 11 per cent in Brazil and 30 per cent in Japan. China's expenditure on education in 1985 was 3.7 per cent of GNP, compared to 5.6 per cent in Japan, and 6.6 per cent in the Soviet Union (3.7 per cent in India and 2.9 per cent in Brazil).

Education, and especially in the fields of science and technology, is now receiving special attention from the Chinese leadership. But the more basic levels of prosperity for the masses are evident in basic health statistics. Despite having half the per capita number of doctors and nurses as India, China, like Brazil, has a significantly higher level of daily calorific intake and one-fifth the number of babies born with a low birth-weight. The life-expectancy in China in 1986 was 69, compared to 57 in India and Indonesia, 65 in Brazil, and 70 in the Soviet Union.

Perhaps the most important uncertainty in projecting these figures towards the future (and for the economy as a whole) is

the rate of population growth. It has only been in the past year
that China has admitted that its upbeat forecasts about being
able to reduce the reproduction rate to one by the year 2000
is optimistic. According to these earlier predictions, China's
population would stabilize at about 1.6 billion, roughly the same
as India's point of stabilization ten years later. That compares
with Nigeria's and Pakistan's stabilization in 2035 at 529 m and
423 m respectively—soon-to-be the world's third and fourth
largest populations. Although China has clearly slipped back
from constituting 25 per cent of the world's population (it will
be about 12 per cent in ten years' time), even a small margin of
error will create havoc for Chinese planners.

Leadership and Legitimacy

It is already clear that many of the failures and fluctuations in
Chinese policies have been closely related to leadership politics.
As leaders and groups wax and wane, they periodically blame
their rivals for past errors and pledge future stability and prosperity. Major figures have been purged with a regularity that
even outdoes the Soviet Union's record. From Gao Gang and
Peng Dehuai in the 1950s, to Liu Shaoqi in the 1960s, Lin Biao
and Jiang Qing in the 1970s and Hu Yaobang in the 1980s, few
top leaders have survived unscathed. Deng Xiaoping himself
has been up and down so many times that his protestations that
all would be stable in the 1980s were never credible.

In the Chinese political system where leadership politics is
so heavily influenced by personal relations, policy does not
necessarily change when leaders do. The fall of Hu Yaobang is
a case in point where the reforms were not seriously affected by
the downfall of one of their most ardent advocates. But in a
country that makes so much about the moral basis of power,
and thus focuses much more on individuals rather than legal
systems, the very legitimacy of the government is challenged
when heads roll so regularly at the top.

Legitimacy is also threatened when policies are shifted as
often as they have been. Therefore, it is not surprising that
Chinese Communists have stretched so far back in their current
efforts at ideological reform that they have come up with the
bizarre concept of 'the primary stage of socialism'.[6] Much like

Mikhail Gorbachev has discovered with greater intensity (because of his faster political reform and slower economic reform), some convincing answer must be provided as to why the Communist Party should be allowed to rule when it has changed its ideas so often.

Ultimately, legitimacy will come from the credibility provided by good government. In the past decade of reform, the Chinese Communists have had a better record than ever before. As a result, the looming problem of legitimacy was held at bay. But the stalling of reform and the resurgence of active factional politics in late 1988, led some to think that the issue of legitimacy is back on the agenda. Why should China be governed by Communists when success elsewhere in Asia has come from much more mildly authoritarian states who mix a command economy with a free market?

A full and frank answer to that question might well lead to another revolution in China. But the revolutionary conditions are not present. We are now in an era of excitable reform when judgements are hasty and reactions often ill-judged. Leaders may change, and policies certainly will, but matters will have to get much worse before there is a determined search for an alternative source of legitimacy. Without a credible opposition, the more likely outcome is moderation and muddle. In the meantime, the rest of the world will move on.

China and the World

If China were in Africa, perhaps it would face less obvious challenges from the outside world. But it is smack in the middle of dynamic East Asia and unless China does sustain quite remarkable growth rates, it is likely to fall even further behind its neighbours. It is still hard to believe that for millennia China was the centre of East Asian civilization and that despite Mao having claimed to have dragged China upright again, it has fallen further behind. The GDP of neighbouring South Korea in 1965 was 4 per cent of that of China, now it is 40 per cent and closing.

To be sure, China now has many more foreign contacts and its foreign trade is rising sharply as the doors are opened to nearly every state in the world. China has abandoned many ideological blinkers and pursues a more pragmatic foreign policy that often staggers the outside observer. It is to China's credit that it has pursued a more sustained line of reform in foreign policy as compared with nearly every other area of policy in the past decade. With normalization of relations with the Soviet Union and Indonesia in 1989, China's position in the international community has never looked better. This, the 'fifth modernization', has become a success.

Yet, much like the verdict on the economy, China's position in the world could have been obtained years earlier. China has changed its foreign policy more dramatically than any other great power and has confused friends and foe alike. It still has some way to go before it is trusted by others as a reliable friend or a stable enemy. The chip on China's shoulder is noticeable and still heavy. It remains uneasy in a world of interdependence whose currency is economic power. China also remains the only great power with unsettled frontiers and unfinished territorial claims. Thus China sees the world in a different light than do most other great powers.

The Challenge of China, to China

Perhaps we should not be churlish on China's birthday by pointing out what it might have achieved if only China had been brighter and luckier. Perhaps it is best not to point to China's deep tragedies and callous errors. Rather it is more fair to praise the achievements of the revolution. China is a stronger, more prosperous, pleasant, and promising place than at any point in many centuries. Although most countries can make a similar claim for their past forty years, few started from such dire straits.

Looking forward a further twenty years is not wise—just think how unlikely it was that anyone would predict China in 1989 would look so different from China at the height of the 'Cultural Revolution' in 1969. Yet at least one American report suggested, before the brick wall of reform was encountered in 1988, that by 2010 China would have the world's second largest GDP and be well established as a poor (on a per capita basis) superpower. Even the Chinese shy away from such flattery and unrealistic extrapolation.

It is more reasonable to say that by the dawn of the supposed Pacific Century in ten-or-so years, China will look much the same. It will be ruled by Communist reformers of one stripe or another. It will have the world's largest population, but remain more a poor-income than a middle-income economy, albeit with major and increasing regional variations. China will also have several open doors to the outside world, and no doubt be involved in as many conflicts as it deals with in 1989. But considering the relative decline of the superpowers and the rise of Japan and the NICs, China will find a new balance of power in Asia. Of course, China will also be a challenge to the outside world. In any case, and more importantly for the well-being of the billion-plus Chinese people, China's inability to formulate a coherent strategy for the future will pose the main challenge to China's own new generation of rulers.

1. These questions have been addressed in different forms in Harry Harding *China's Second Revolution* (Washington: Brookings, 1987) and David S. G. Goodman, Martin Lockett, Gerald Segal, *The China Challenge* (London: Chatham House Papers published by Routledge, 1987).
2. These figures are drawn from *World Development Report 1988* of the World Bank. But a Chinese report in the *Beijing Review*, 30 January 1989, noted that currency rates mask all sorts of changes. In terms of yuan, Chinese GNP was up 2.25 times in the 1978–87 period when calculated in 1980 prices. But when converted into US dollars at the 1980 exchange rate, China's GNP turns out to be 10 per cent lower in the same period. For similar reasons, China's GNP fell from a quarter of that of Japan in 1980 to one-fifth in 1985 and one-sixth in 1986. A RAND study, using the inexact calculations of purchasing-power-equivalents, found Chinese GNP to be higher than suggested in the figures above and estimated that China's total GNP will have surpassed that of Japan by the year 2010.
3. Louise do Rosario in *Far Eastern Economic Review*, 2 March 1989, p. 48.
4. For a balanced, but favourable view see Cyril Lin 'China's Economy: The Aspiration and the Reality', in *The World Today*, January 1989.
5. For a recent articulation see 'Keeping up with the New China' in *New York Review of Books*, 16 March 1989.
6. These issues are discussed by David S. G. Goodman in 'The Importance of China's 13th Party Congress', *The Pacific Review* No. 1, 1988.

1. Marxism and Reformism

TERRELL CARVER and LI JUN

RECENT articles in the Chinese press reflect the theoretical debates that inevitably accompany practical reforms in China. Unsurprisingly there is considerable stress there in accommodating radical ideas within an established Marxist doctrine. To some extent the necessity to work within communist ideology is a prerequisite that is politically enforced, but it is also true that alternative frameworks simply have no hold in a country where for forty years intellectual pluralism has been disallowed. For that reason the debates are a serious matter within the ruling party and beyond to a larger audience, as they represent the only way that differing views can be stated and defended. An analysis of these debates can show outsiders not only what is now at stake but also how future policy positions may coalesce. Marxist ideology and reference to Marx's texts in China are no mere façade and should not be ignored or discounted. There are power struggles and personality politics in the West, but few academics would argue that they should be studied independently of the unwritten conventions of parliamentary democracy and the great constitutional texts and commentaries. The situation in China is little different.

What is surprising about current debates in China is the extent to which the traditional methodological framework and substantive doctrines of Marxism are being stretched almost out of recognition. The way that this is happening is of interest to Marxist and non-Marxist audiences elsewhere, as the economic problems under consideration and the solutions proposed have an almost universal application in the modern world. But the way that Marx is being re-read in China can only be fully appreciated against a background of western scholarship on Marx, which has—over the last twenty years—drastically changed the way that his writings are interpreted. Some of this western work on Marx has filtered into China, and we may now be seeing the results.

Realistic Socialism

The issues occupying Hong Zhaolong in his article 'Necessary to "Restudy Capitalism" because of "Mistakes" in Works of Lenin, Marx, Engels' (Beijing, *Guangming Ribao*, 29 February 1988) are clearly related to questions concerning the reform of the Chinese economy and the development of what he terms 'realistic socialism'. He suggests that 'realistic socialism' could well incorporate elements from contemporary capitalism, such as the production of commodities for the market, and even the exploitation of labour. From that sort of reform he evidently expects China to reap benefits already attained in capitalist countries—rapid development of the economy and a universal improvement in the material and cultural life of society. Indeed his 'realistic socialism' could also include elements of 'bourgeois democracy' and law, because in his view these political institutions have been improved as the class struggle in capitalist countries has been mitigated. In the ideological and cultural fields some aspects of modern capitalist society are reasonable and useful, he says, and these transcend the limitations of different social systems—even the strictures of time and space! Knowing the extent to which these highly controversial ideas run counter to traditional materialist and dialectical Marxism, Hong Zhaolong urges his readers to emulate the 'courage shown by Marx and Engels when they revised the conclusion[s] of the "Manifesto" [to] face reality'.

The 'courageous' Marx is revealed by Hong Zhaolong to be the Marx who revised and corrected the 1848 Communist 'Manifesto' in his later years. This 'courageous' Marx is far removed by implication from a hypothetical cowardly Marx who would have treated his own works dogmatically and would never have considered revising or correcting them. The dogmatic, ever-correct Marx is clearly intended to be the Marx revered by traditionalists—stalwarts of the planned economy and opponents of contemporary economic reform. The consequences of traditional Marxism, according to Hong Zhaolong, were stagnation in the consumer sector and slow economic growth overall.

It is quite true, as Hong Zhaolong points out, that Marx revised his views concerning the necessity for violent revolution by the proletariat in order to achieve socialism, or at least the preliminary stages of it, and quite true that he wrote approvingly of a possibility for peaceful revolution in Britain, Holland and the United States. But the question for Hong Zhaolong—and for us—is how any analysis of contemporary politics that claims to follow Marx's ideas, or to revise them in a way consistent with the thrust of his work, could possibly generate a convincing justification for the 'realistic socialism' that Hong Zhaolong is keen to promote. In another recent article in the Chinese press, 'Scientific Socialism and Modern Capitalism Both Develop the Productive Forces' (Beijing, *Guangming Ribao*, 15 February 1988), Gao Fang tackles the same problem. Though he interprets the 'Manifesto' rather differently, he still arrives at the same impasse.

Socialist Public Ownership

Hong Zhaolong based his defence of economic reform on his claims that the 'Manifesto' requires revision and that Marx set a good example by revising it himself. By contrast Gao Fang's argument is drawn from the 'Manifesto' as Marx left it. Gao Fang's view is that the proletariat can seize political power and use it to develop productive forces in the economy, and he points to the fact that the 'Manifesto' contains virtually the same argument with respect to commercial classes emerging in feudal society. Just as they battled to remove power from the clerical and secular lords of feudalism, in order to develop the productive forces already available, so the proletariat, in Gao Fang's view, must devote huge efforts to developing their productive forces *after* a proletarian seizure of power. Attempting socialism, without undertaking this development of the mode of production, merely repeats the error that Marx condemned in the utopian socialists, but without the excuse that utopian failures were still of some value as markers for the future. In Gao Fang's view the utility of such markers is long past, because the possibility for 'genuine production relations of socialist public ownership' is now at hand.

Gao Fang interprets the 'Manifesto' in a way that reflects contemporary western interpretations of Marx, rather than orthodox Marxism. This is because Gao Fang does not rely on well-worn notions of determinism and causation, mind and matter, materialism and idealism, base and superstructure, science and truth, dialectics and evolutionary development—as does the more traditional Hong Zhaolong. Instead Gao Fang connects the concept of productive forces, emphasized by Marx himself, directly with the activity of individuals, and then with class-activity. Interestingly for Gao Fang the concept of class-activity as he derives it from Marx is not synonymous with class-struggle. Gao Fang argues that an ascendant proletariat has no class to battle against, so the struggles of the 1960s and 1970s in China were therefore frankly a mistake. Instead the real activity facing the Chinese proletariat today, as then, is the development of productive forces with all due speed, and for guidance he is clearly looking West.

Though Gao Fang's Marx is a more flexible and sophisticated social theorist than Hong Zhaolong's, the two Chinese writers reach similar conclusions. This is because they both view western capitalism as substantially reformed in itself, and both argue that reformism in China should follow suit. Gao Fang's 'socialist public ownership' is not far removed from Hong Zhaolong's 'realistic socialism'. But their common conclusion is in fact very close to the view that whatever facilitates the rapid expansion of Chinese productive forces is *by definition* a desirable mitigation of class struggle *and* a nascent form of socialism. Their enthusiasm for the social changes that have occurred in capitalist societies since Marx's time—separation of ownership from operational rights in enterprises, the increasing importance of managers as opposed to capitalist investors, the vastly increased role of the state in regulating economic and cultural life, improvements in working conditions, even electronic democracy—gives the lie to their ritual genuflection to the defects of capitalism outlined by Marx—class antagonism, class polarization, economic crises, exploitation and unemployment. Certainly both Chinese writers see little point in applying Marx's ideas to a critical analysis of contemporary capitalism in the West, and once they have taken that position, their tendency to look to contemporary western economics for guidance on social policy in China can then proceed without serious challenge.

Marx as an Obstacle to Reform

Current western scholarship has emphasized Marx's role as a critic of capitalism, the originator of theories of 'alienation' and 'exploitation'. The preceding traditional view of Marx—

popularized by Marxists and anti-Marxists alike—was that he acted as a scientist-philosopher, presenting an overarching theory of 'dialectical materialism' that can be applied to 'history'. Perhaps our two Chinese writers are really saying that Marx, with his newly emphasized concepts of class struggle and communist society, and traditional Marxism, with its mish-mash of philosophy and science, are both obstacles to reform. Chinese political theorists are evidently thinking very radical thoughts, almost unthinkable ones, as they turn from Marx and Marxism towards market-oriented western economics. This extraordinary vitality can also be observed in the current practical experiments with economic reform in China.

China is now opening itself to western ideas and practices. But the openness of today is very different from that of 150 years ago when China was forced by foreign invaders to open its doors. The Chinese Communist Party took power in 1949, but due to historical circumstances, such as the Korean War and the Sino-Soviet dispute, it was cut off for three decades. Only in December 1978, at the Third Plenum of the Central Committee of the Eleventh Chinese Communist Party Congress, did Chinese leaders become determined to catch up with economically advanced countries.

It is unlikely that the 'Manifesto' or any other text by Marx was the primary inspiration for this policy, as his emphasis was primarily on the criticism of capitalist society and the encouragement of the class struggle. The Marxist tradition, derived most obviously from Soviet sources, provides some explicit justification for rapid economic expansion under a planned economy, but those ideologues associated with market-oriented policies were declared anathema by Stalin and thus became dubious candidates for ideological authority. The connection between the reconstruction of the Soviet economy to incorporate market principles and the current round of rehabilitations, most notably Bukharin's, is obvious. But it seems likely that Chinese Marxists will prefer their independent approach, returning to Marx's basic works to attempt to justify their current reformist line on the economy. As Marx was not a notable advocate of markets, this is a tricky exercise in finding views that will *allow* an emphasis of market-led growth in building socialism, for there is no explicit justification for such policies.

Hong Zhaolong does this by pointing to Marx's revisions to his own work and then condemning the methods of dogmatic Stalinism by implication. Gao Fang achieves the same aim by using the 'Manifesto' to construct a conception of class-activity that contradicts Stalinist dogmas on the role of the planned economy in socialism. Since Marx did not pronounce in detail on the exact procedures for building socialism, the exercise might seem to be promising. But to undertake it commentators must work hard to avoid the subject on which Marx was most voluble—the defects of the market economy under capitalism.

In Marx's analysis the market is itself the basic flaw underneath all others in capitalist society. He argued that the introduction of money to facilitate exchange was a revolution in human history, in that it provided a workable scheme of incentives to promote production. But it also required individuals to see each other as isolated or separate entities whose interests were necessarily opposed because each is the proprietor of private property. It was precisely this historically created relation of isolation and mutual opposition that Marx's communism was supposed to remedy through a system of planned production—a system which never progressed, in Marx's hands, beyond a mere statement of intent. Thus in his work, and in the Marxist heritage, there is a basic objection in principle to monetary exchange on the market, and that analysis of commodity-exchange is at the root of the communist attack on the market and on capitalist societies. The creation of some form of market socialism requires a fundamental revision of Marx's work, rather than a mere re-interpretation of certain lines in the 'Manifesto'.

The Role of Ideology

One of the most striking features of Chinese communists is that in the past they regarded ideology as of supreme importance. However in China Marxist ideology was understood mainly through Soviet textbooks of the 1930s that were written under the influence of Stalin, hence Hong Zhaolong's revisionist defence of the 'courageous', non-dogmatic Marx. Many mistakes were made in China as a result of Stalinist Marxism, and these brought disasters time and again to the country's development.

For instance, people were taught to think that they were living in a time of revolution, so it was important for them to support world revolution instead of developing the country's economy. Moreover, forced collectivization in the countryside brought increased bureaucracy and further insufficiency. To make things worse, the market mechanism was condemned as a phenomenon of capitalism. There were political movements continuously revolutionizing the people in order to put 'politics in command', so the backwardness of the country was ignored.

At the Third Plenum of the Central Committee in December 1978, the Party got rid of those outdated restraints, shifting the focus from class struggle to socialist modernization. Economic reform, including openness to the outside world, was set in motion. Since then the Chinese have gradually liberated themselves from what Marx, Engels or Lenin said and wrote, because many of their comments and conclusions were based on the circumstances of the nineteenth and early twentieth centuries. With the advance of modern science and technology, the contemporary world has changed dramatically, so Chinese leaders have repeatedly called for the creative application of Marxism. Hong Zhaolong and Gao Fang have taken precisely this view in arguing that the economic development of western capitalism has vitiated much of Marx's critique of the market, however appropriate it was to his own time. Their view seems to be that in so far as Marx's work is compatible with the changed nature of capitalism, and in so far as it does not stand in the way of the socialist development of productive forces by whatever means, it is worth citing as a justification for current policies and as a source of political inspiration. But in so far as it is now, however regrettably, incompatible with their assessment of the needs of Chinese socialism, it should be relegated to the museum.

On matters of political tactics in the class struggle Marx was an open advocate of revision, as and when required, and no friend of a dogmatic approach. Most famously his view of correct proletarian strategy during the 1848 events themselves underwent a reversal—from a united front with middle-class constitutionalism to a complete separation of the proletarian party. As the revolutionary struggle developed, the middle classes, in Marx's view, engaged in perfidious compromises with reactionaries that were inimical to workers' interests—hence the strategic *volte face* as workers were advised to defend themselves from their class enemies as best they could. But the revisions that Hong Zhaolong advocates in current Chinese economic policy are not of this tactical character.

On points of social science, such as the analysis and evaluation of the market and monetary exchange, Marx admitted the possibility of correction in principle. But his arguments were tightly constructed and never subjected in his lifetime to an informal critique. From his point of view there was little reason to doubt them, and he proudly considered them to be well founded in experience and hence scientific in character. Gao Fang attempts to sidestep the difficulties of criticizing these fundamental arguments concerning the market by appealing directly to Marx's concept of productive activity, and arguing that the market mechanism has a place within a proletarian economy. It is difficult to imagine any reaction to this on Marx's part but sheer horror, and similarly for Marxists, still dedicated in principle to the planned economy. Gao Fang's work is an attempt to finesse the market within the framework established by Marx. Now that the planned economy is disgraced almost everywhere as an engine of economic production, the market has become the only credible alternative—and a place for it will be established within the Marxist camp. Western scholarship reveals, on the one hand, how difficult a job this is, and on the other, the points where these difficulties can be avoided and some sort of Marx-like analysis constructed in order to meet the political and intellectual requirements of Marxist countries, most notably China.

2. State Administration and Economic Reform

MARC BLECHER

A central feature of China's programme of economic modernization since 1978 has been a redefinition of the role of the state *vis-à-vis* the economy, which has included the organization and activities of state administration.[1] It has taken two directions which may be distinguished analytically, although in theory they are not mutually exclusive—indeed, they may be complementary—and in practice they may overlap. One is the separation of state administrative structures and activities from the economy, the other the reorientation of such administration in ways more consistent with effective management of the economy. The former has included administrative streamlining, increasing managers' authority and independence from state officials, reducing state agencies' financial leverage over enterprises, allowing enterprises to be dissolved through bankruptcy, and reform of investment finance through the creation of an independent banking system. The latter has included meritocratic personnel reform (so state officials will be better qualified to run the economy), the separation of Party from government, and the effort to reorient the role of state officials in the economy.

Separation of State and Economy

If one cause of the great expansion of the state administrative apparatus in China after 1949 was the socialist transformation of the economy to centralized control, the reverse has not occurred. Despite all the steps toward privatization, expanded market relations, decentralization and deregulation, the sheer number of people in the Chinese state actually grew by 72 per cent (by 3,015,000 people!) between 1978 and 1984, a period when China's population grew by only 7 per cent. A Party circular issued as recently as May 1988 continued to urge 'government streamlining', an indication that the problem of administrative bloat continues.

There are at least six reasons for this. First, since 1978 a huge contingent—doubtless into seven figures—of officials who had been evicted from their positions during the Cultural Revolution decade was officially rehabilitated and returned to former units to work alongside those who had taken their places.

Second, the policy of encouraging older officials to retire was largely a failure, for at least three reasons. Firstly, it contradicted the policy of rehabilitation. Those denounced during the Cultural Revolution did not want to go through the difficult process of rehabilitation in order to find themselves immediately retired. Moreover, if rehabilitated officials would be retired anyway, there would be no incentive for their units to take rehabilitation work seriously. Secondly, officials could not feel sure they would have their medical, financial and housing needs met if they retired, since in China these are still provided by work units, not social services programmes. Thirdly, the private, passive life of retirement was not an attractive prospect to officials who had spent active lives in the pursuit and acquisition of power in the public realm.

Third, no effort was made to restructure the Chinese bureaucracy. The coexistence of dual systems of leadership—vertically-organized ministries and mass organizations, their bureaux and sub-units at each level, the Communist Party organs paralleling and embedded in all of them, and then the horizontal organs such as local governments, planning commissions, and Party committees—which had contributed to bureaucratic bloating and much administrative confusion in the first three decades of the People's Republic was not changed. Nor was any effort made to rationalize the provision of government services. Since social services were still dispensed largely by production units, not specialized agencies, there were continuing problems of duplication of work and of the personnel to do it.

Fourth, it continued to be in the interests of administrative agencies to retain as large a staff as possible. Despite all the attacks on Chinese political culture and administrative practice, it has remained the case that the larger the unit, the more prestigious it is and the more powerful its leaders. Large units are also better positioned for elevation in the bureaucratic hierarchy, which is a pathway to increased income, prestige and power for their leaders and members.

A fifth factor has to do with educational changes. The number of graduates of tertiary institutions has exploded starting in 1982, when 457,000 received their degrees—more than twice as many as the previous high of 194,000 (in 1977). In 1983–85, an average of 313,000 per year graduated. The government was faced with the task of finding employment for all these people, and many—probably most—were placed in administrative posts.

Sixth, and perhaps most important, the economic and political reforms have themselves promoted administrative growth. The rapid expansion and diversification of the Chinese economy since 1978 have called for a larger and more ramified administrative structure. Compared with 1978, there are now many more train tickets to sell, units from which to collect taxes, roads to build, markets to regulate, housing units to construct and administer, technologies to develop and oversee, types and numbers of consumer goods to supply, and so forth. Political reforms have had the same effect. The elaboration of more complex forms of property and the increasing importance of property rights, along with the general expansion of law and the judicial system, have promoted the development of new legal agencies and administrative tasks. The transfer of local security personnel from the military to local governments has also added to the size of administrative payrolls. So has the assignment of demobilized soldiers to government positions as part of the streamlining of the armed forces.

Administrative expansion has gone hand in hand with increased administrative expenditure. In 1969, the government spent 2,982,000,000 yuan on administration, a figure which increased gradually to 4,518,000,000 yuan by 1977, for an average rate of growth of 5.33 per cent per year. Beginning in 1978, administrative expenditure began a new and much higher average rate of increase of 17 per cent per year, reaching 11,572,000,000 yuan in 1983.[2] Whereas in 1977, 4.1 per cent of total government expenditures went to administration, by 1983 this more than doubled to 9 per cent.

The size and cost of government administration have grown

dramatically since the advent of the Chinese reforms. This does not by itself necessarily mean that the state is more closely, directly or heavily involved in the economy. But it certainly does not bode well for a separation of state and economy. In a developing socialist country like China, where the vast majority of economic activity is still owned, managed and administered by the state, where the economy is still the major preoccupation of the state, where economic modernization is the explicit policy of the present regime, the rapid growth of the state bureaucracy can only mean that more officials will be well positioned, inclined and expected to exert power over the economy.

Reform of the State Sector

It was not until almost six years into the reform period that a major programmatic statement on the reform of state sector enterprise was made.[3] A key element was the manager responsibility system. But the 'Decision' withheld from the managers the authority which this 'full responsibility' would have to entail. The functions of Party control and enterprise management were not clearly differentiated. The 'Decision' was no decision at all. It was a grab-bag of statements which could be used by all those involved in state sector enterprises to justify their policy positions, pursuit of interests, and exercise of power.

The result has been something of a free-for-all. Where managers were able to assert themselves, some engaged in practices that are questionable from a socialist point of view. They hired former 'class enemies', many of whom were precisely the entrepreneurial sorts required by the reform programme. They engaged in illegal trade, for example by purchasing equipment or materials at low state prices and reselling them on the black market. They increased their own salaries. Some with the appropriate access imported large quantities of foreign goods for resale at high profits, and made fortunes from black market exchanges of Chinese currency.

Yet in other places managers were tightly constrained by state officials. They were frequently denied the personal authority to hire, promote or transfer—not to mention fire—their immediate subordinates. This undercut their ability to function as modern firm directors as well as their political power in their enterprises (which of course they would need to deepen their authority as managers). In a compromise, they have gained the capacity to hire some middle- and lower-level supervisory personnel.

The resulting personnel situation provides a context for several different kinds of conflict. Where these supervisory personnel are indeed committed to increased efficiency and therefore discipline the labour force more closely, worker discontent has followed, and found expression partly in a recent wave of strikes, slowdowns and production sabotage.[4] Both in the enterprises—where state officials are still strong—and the wider political system, these have played into the hands of critics of thoroughgoing reform. Conflicts between state—particularly Party—officials and managers have been widely reported, some so serious as to be characterized as 'civil wars'. The managers are not well placed to win them: 'Young factory managers . . . are often forced to resign because of local hostility to their new ways.'[5]

Though objections to the manager responsibility system are usually couched in ideological terms such as the need to preserve socialism's commitment to Party control, workers' interests, or democratic management (themselves often contradictory goals), they are rooted in the concerns of state officials about their loss of power or even function if authority in enterprises is turned over to managers. These anxieties are only heightened by Party officials' experiences of being shunted aside during the Cultural Revolution. Put more positively, they did not fight to be rehabilitated from the political eclipse of those years only to yield their newly refound position, influence and power to factory managers.

In general, too, there tend to be deep differences in outlook between state officials and factory managers. Many of the former attained their positions during the revolution or the immediate post-revolutionary period, while managers tend to have been recruited and educated in the 1950s, 1960s and even 1970s. A correlate of this is that managers tend to be younger and better educated than state officials. They have usually been recruited on the basis of their education, whereas state officials' career pathways came through political, administrative or military posts. So there is good reason to expect sharp disagreements among them on matters of enterprise management and the role of the enterprise in a socialist country. Neither the 'Decision' discussed above nor the more recently promulgated Enterprise Law could resolve them.[6] In fact, according to a Party circular, the Enterprise Law was intended to address 'the lack of separation . . . of government administration and enterprise management . . . [which] is still a major obstacle to making enterprises more productive and profitable'.[7] Yet this piece of legislation continued to equivocate, subjecting managers' authority over pay schemes to approval by Workers' Congresses, and leaving with local government departments the power to 'issue unified mandatory plans for the enterprises' and to 'appoint or remove, reward or punish the factory director . . . [and] the leading administrative cadres at the level of vice-director'. The Chinese press is still admitting and complaining that the problem of separating the state administration from management is unresolved.

To the extent that the differences between managers and state officials have to do with essentially generational differences, they may fade away with the passing of time, leaving China with a technocratic corps of leaders at the enterprise level. Indeed, this is already beginning to happen. A factory manager in Wenzhou, a locality now at the epicentre of reform, has hired his friend to serve as the Party secretary of the enterprise, in order to help him deal with problems the local government posed for the firm. This example shows that such arrangements are as likely to produce perverse new mergers of state and economy as they are to separate them. Indeed, to the extent that a more unified generation of technocrats dominates positions in the state administration and the enterprises, there is a strong possibility that it could form an integrated political–economic leadership or even élite.

There is another deep contradiction lurking in the manager responsibility system. As Hong Yung Lee has recently pointed out, 'In . . . management method, the [Party] secretary uses the "soft" method of persuasion even if it takes a long time. In contrast, the managers use the "hard method" of administrative orders or economic rewards'.[8] Managers' reliance on administrative fiat stands in direct opposition to the political liberalization which is another prominent aspect of reform. Thus, it may come under criticism from those reform leaders and social groups who are deeply concerned with political change. To the extent that it does, it may put pressure on the very diverse and potentially fragile social coalition which has backed reform during its first decade.

The Substitution of Taxes for Profits

Reformers recognized early on that state enterprises would have little incentive to increase productivity or raise profits so long as the state claimed all or most enterprise profits. So one of the first reform moves was the adjustment of profit remission ratios so that the enterprises could keep more of them. This led to several problems. Enterprises proved adroit at negotiating low remission rates with the bureaux that supervised them. In turn, this meant that local state officials spent a great deal of time and effort dickering; profit remission rates were neither standardized nor set according to criteria that were rational economically (such as structural constraints facing the enterprise or sector) or politically (such as leadership priorities about development); and, in general, state revenues declined. It also left the central government agencies at the mercy of local ones, which had the power to negotiate the low retention rates whose ultimate financial consequences had to be dealt with centrally.

Beginning experimentally in 1983 and then widely promulgated in 1984, the leadership attempted to solve these problems by replacing profit remissions with taxes. It was argued that these would be more standard, predictable and useful as a lever of macroeconomic regulation. Moreover, since enterprises would now be submitting their surpluses to the highly centralized Ministry of Finance and Taxation, local governments would lose financial leverage over or benefit from local enterprises. This in turn would enhance the latter's autonomy from government administration. Since the state was no longer collecting profits, the enterprises could now also be held fully accountable for their after-tax profits and losses, which would give them an incentive to increase their autonomy. Between 1983 and 1987, Chinese leaders and their press repeatedly sang the praises of the new tax system.

They were so heavily committed to it that when they decided to drop it in 1987, they did so with no public fanfare, evaluation or criticism of it whatsoever. They did not wish to advertise this major victory for local governments, who had militated against the tax policy precisely because it had reduced their power over enterprises under their supervision. Political pressure aside, the replacement of profit remissions with taxes probably did not deliver everything it promised in terms of increased regularity of revenues and enterprise autonomy. An official of the Guanghan County Finance and Tax Bureau said in late 1986: 'Now the system of three distinct types of state, collective and private ownership has been replaced by many more mixed forms. So it's difficult to know which taxes and tax rates apply to a particular enterprise. The regulations can't be clear. It's up to us to decide'. Clearly this local government bureau was able to exercise significant leverage over local enterprises.

The system of taxes replacing profits was supplanted by a system called profit contracting, under which 'state owned enterprises which are able to make profits must fulfill an annual set quota of profits and increase it each year at a regular rate. The enterprises then share with the State the amount made in excess of the quota'.[9] It is difficult to see much difference between this system and the old profit remission system, which had been criticized for allowing too much local government influence over enterprises' finances. At present financial relationships between enterprises and the state are in disarray, with a proliferation of local practices. The state, though critical of them for not serving its interests and allowing 'government departments to interfere too much in enterprises' economic decisions and routine affairs, is justifying inaction in the name of continued experimentation.

Bankruptcy

Beginning in February 1985, the industrial city of Shenyang began to moot bankruptcy as an approach to making enterprises autonomous and responsible for their own affairs. Though no bankruptcy law yet existed, in September 1986 the Shenyang Explosion-Proof Equipment Factory, which was unable to pay off 503,000 yuan in debts (against assets of only 302,000 yuan), was the first Chinese firm to be declared bankrupt since 1949. It was sold to the Shenyang Gas Supply Company at an auction that attracted thirty bidders. Its seventy-two workers were laid off, though disabled workers and those near retirement received benefits of three-quarters of their salaries for an unspecified period.[10]

This approach to enterprise policy caused a storm of controversy in China. Proponents argued that only if enterprises faced the possibility of bankruptcy would they take responsibility for themselves seriously and strive to make prudent investments and management decisions. Opponents on the Standing Committee of the National People's Congress argued against it on several grounds. First, it was premature to pass a bankruptcy law until legislation on workers' rights and unemployment insurance were in place. Second, it was unfair to hold enterprises responsible for their losses in this most draconian manner so long as local governments were still exercising power over them. Third, so long as prices remained unreformed, enterprise profits or losses were often poor indicators of their efficiency and productivity. Away from the pinnacles of power, workers complained that they ought not to have to suffer the economic hardship and 'shame' of unemployment because of the poor management of the plant. For local governments, bankruptcies would create a host of problems: adding more workers to the already swollen rolls of unemployed job-seekers, putting financial pressure on local social services (as workers would become unable to meet their medical, housing or children's school expenses), and generally increasing local discontent whose expression could cause political and security problems.

In the face of these difficulties and controversies, the state equivocated. The Eighteenth Session of the Sixth National People's Congress Standing Committee decided in November 1986 to approve a tentative draft of a bankruptcy law for trial implementation in a small number of units. And while some sabres continued to be rattled through the early part of 1987, bankruptcy has been shelved for the moment (though there are hints that it may be making a comeback).

In 1988, it was replaced by a new approach under which unprofitable firms were absorbed into profitable ones. This created new problems. Most significantly, by permitting local governments to allocate the assets of one enterprise to another, it actually increased their power *vis-à-vis* enterprises, thereby mitigating against the separation of government administration from enterprises, which was one of the original, overarching goals of the bankruptcy policy in the first place. In addition, it saddled the enterprises into which unprofitable firms were absorbed with large contingents of new workers whose labour could not be used efficiently but for whom payrolls still had to be met. In what may be an indication of ongoing controversy over this approach, in August 1988 the press again began to mention bankruptcy. But in the environment of much more cautious economic policy and political apprehension which followed immediately thereafter, centred around deep back-pedalling on price reform, any offensive on bankruptcy seems unlikely.

Banking Reform

A major effort to free the economy from government interference, and to have key decisions made on economic rather than political grounds, has centred around banking reform. The banking system has been elaborated, strengthened and in theory made more autonomous from the state. All enterprises, including those in the state sector, now have to seek capital from banks, not ministries as in the past. And banks have been instructed to operate according to strict economic principles in evaluating requests for credit.

The problem is that at the middle and lower levels such as in the provinces and in particular counties, where the actual financial decisions take place, the banks have not been autonomous of local state organs, and have not or have been unable to operate according to economic criteria alone in regulating and distributing credit. Under pressure from local governments and enterprises for financial support of their development plans or pet projects, or simply to keep existing enterprises with their large labour forces afloat, banks have been exceeding their quotas in extending new loans. Consequently the money supply has expanded out of control.

The central leadership has responded in two ways. First, it has sought to constrict the dispensation of bank credit. But this is difficult to do. It involves centralization of political control over a key sector of the economy, which goes against the decentralizing and pro-market thrusts of the reforms. So long as the banks are not themselves responsible in a serious way for their own profits and losses, there is little sanction behind central regulatory efforts. Moreover, if the banks really are given the opportunity to make profits, they may expand their lending even further, which contradicts the need to slow the excessive rate of economic expansion and investment. Still, there may be some room for the state to use its control over the careers of bankers to discipline the way they dispense credit. However, this would require personnel policies which have been difficult to implement, as we shall see. It might also be possible to restructure the banking system in a way which makes it more truly autonomous of local state organs—for example, as a kind of separate and independent government corporation. However, so far such corporations in the productive sphere have proved to be nothing more than the same old enterprises dressed up under new names.

Second, there have been experiments with private banking, highly publicized as the 'Wenzhou model' after the city in Zhejiang Province where private banking has mushroomed. Privatization of banking poses its own very serious problems. In Wenzhou, private banks threaten stiff competition for the state banks, which in turn can be expected to bring political pressure to bear within the state to regulate or restrict them. The higher interest rates they pay and charge tend to fuel inflation, about which the leadership has recently been so apprehensive that it backed down on a long-promised price reform. As already noted, a profit-oriented banking sector would probably only magnify the problem of excessive investment rates in China's overheated economy.

Prospects

In conclusion, efforts at state sector economic reform intended to separate the state from enterprises and enhance the autonomy of the latter have by and large met with failure. The effort to grant managers fuller responsibility for their enterprises has proceeded unevenly and uncertainly. Where it has been implemented, it has tended to produce technocratic élitism which does not get the state out of enterprises but only transforms its mode of insertion into them. And increased managerial power poses a serious contradiction with political reform too, by making enterprises more authoritarian. Attempts to use taxation to deprive local governments of the financial power they garnered by appropriating enterprise profits have met with such serious political opposition and poor results that they had to be reversed. Bankruptcy, another way of making enterprises responsible for their own finances, has to date gone nowhere too. And the attempt to use financial levers to reduce political control of the economy and promote economic rationality therein has been difficult to implement, while also contributing to economic overheating and inflation. Thus far, then, removing the state from the administration of state enterprises has proven impossible in some places and problematical in others.

This suggests that the only way to get the state out of the economy is to eliminate or at least attack state ownership itself. It appears that many leaders and scholars in China are beginning to think this way. First, there has been a raging debate on the transformation of state ownership into a kind of joint stock ownership. However, the conceptual ambiguities, theoretical conundra and practical problems of such a development are very great and have not yet been adequately thought through, much less tackled in practice even on a serious trial basis.

Second, there recently seems to have been a clear commitment among China's leadership to expanding the collective and private sectors and restricting further expansion of the state sector. However, there are numerous problems in basing China's economic future on these sectors. Continuing political and administrative obstacles to and harassment of private businesses, combined with ongoing anxiety about a change in the state's policy on or attitude toward the private sector, have induced many private firms to camouflage themselves as collective firms. This has confused the situation and opened many private entrepreneurs to charges of embezzlement when they have tried to claim their private profits from an ostensibly collective firm.

Third, collective sector firms have been frequently criticized for being serious polluters, for their technical backwardness and inefficiency, their proclivity to high or at least unregulated investment, and their exploitative labour practices (such as child labour or the reappearance of the 'forbidden stitch' which induces blindness in embroiderers).

Finally, state-sector firms still dominate the Chinese economy, in 1987 producing 60 per cent of industrial output value (and much higher percentages in key sectors such as steel and energy), employing more than half the urban labour force, taking 85 per cent of urban fixed investment, and accounting for 85 per cent of remissions of industrial profits and taxes. So it is unlikely that this sector could soon become dwarfed by a burgeoning collective, much less private, sector.

If the state sector is here to stay at least for the foreseeable future, and if previous efforts to remove state control over it have failed, what next? At the time of writing, there are a few new wisps in the air intended to revitalize the state sector and diminish state control over it. Recently state firms have been encouraged to emulate the scrappy business tactics of rural collective firms. This avenue seems unpromising at best. The advice is inappropriate: a large power or steel mill cannot be run with the flexibility and hard-nosed management style of a village workshop. Moreover, in general, exhortation doesn't go very far any more in China, if it ever did. Share holding, under which enterprises and workers would own minority shares of their enterprises, was making something of a comeback in policy circles in the spring of 1988 though, as noted earlier, many theoretical problems and practical details remain to be worked out and trial runs undertaken. Bankruptcy was also mooted again briefly in August 1988, though the time for so bold a move seems to have passed for the moment. If a way can be found to make state banks more truly autonomous of other state agencies, finance may be one area where further progress could be made in reducing political influence in the economy.

That aside, there appears little prospect of a significant new approach either to downgrading the state sector or to removing the power of the state from it. China will probably have to face up to the fact that the real question—the one to which there may be feasible answers—is not whether to have a state sector or how to get the state out of it, but rather how to restructure the relationship of the state to it in ways which promote the leadership's goals of economic modernization.

Restructuring of the Relationship Between the State and the Economy

Personnel Policy: Toward Meritocracy?

A necessary condition for such restructuring is the professionalization of state personnel. Recruitment of a better educated leadership possessing more experience with modern technology and methods of management would help promote economic modernization. So would the allocation of rewards and promotions according to performance in promoting modernization. Hence the reform leadership undertook a major 'rectification' of the Party beginning in 1983, and has floated the idea of creating a depoliticized civil service to replace the highly politicized cadre corps that now administers state affairs.

Raising the educational level of the Party has been a daunting task. By the mid-1980s, 42 per cent of Party members still had just a primary education, and another 30 per cent had only finished junior high school. The Party rectification had mainly political objectives, and thus was not concerned directly with removing poorly educated people from the Party. Moreover, it has proven increasingly difficult to attract intellectuals into the Party, because of the Party's low prestige, the fact that Party membership is no longer essential for career success or improved material life, the relatively greater attractiveness of and demands made by professional work, and the intellectuals' justified concern that those with lingering doubts about reform may be more heavily concentrated in the Party than in other state institutions. Still, intellectuals whom the Party does attract will tend to exert greater influence than other new recruits, because of the Party's commitment to promote them quickly to positions of authority.

Recruitment, evaluation and promotion of non-Party officials is still undertaken in ways which do not emphasize professional qualification. Appointments are made by the immediately superior administrative agency and Party committee.[11] While the reform leadership urges that competence be taken into account as one factor, it has neither provided any concrete, objective ways of measuring this nor done more than exhort. Experiments with elections of officials by the members of the units in which they are to serve have tended further to politicize recruitment rather than result in selection of the most educationally or technically qualified persons. Here then is another contradiction between administrative and political reform. And according to *Questions and Answers on Party Organizational Work*, a major reform statement on personnel policy, evaluation and promotion of government as well as Party cadres is still handled by Party committees, which were to use a list of criteria that began with 'virtue *(de)*, focusing on political standpoint and character'.[12]

Promotion and demotion could pose a problem that might be termed a reforming state socialist version of the Peter Principle. In a strongly hierarchical statist system such as that which still exists in China, it is still presumed that power accretes upward. Thus it would make sense for reformers concerned with personnel competence to promote the most qualified and demote the least qualified. But since the reform project is simultaneously decentralizing economic power downward to enterprises, such a personnel policy might tend to demote some of the least competent persons from administrative posts in the bureaucracy to the enterprises, which is precisely the level where competence is most needed. Likewise, it might promote the most technically qualified or entrepreneurial persons out of the enterprises into bureaucratic posts where their skills are less useful.

One approach to personnel problems which has been frequently mooted and hotly debated in China is the creation of a civil service. Aside from its unpopularity among the large phalanx of poorly educated officials who stand to lose out, there are several other problems involved in establishing such a personnel structure in China. There has been no agreement on a job classification system, which is a necessary prerequisite for any civil service. In China's highly politicized state, it is a conceptually as well as politically formidable task to distinguish administrative posts (which would be included in a civil service) from political ones (which would not). And even if this distinction could be made, the job of classifying and then grading administrative posts promises to be nothing less than a practical and, more important, a political nightmare. There are good reasons, then, why proposals for a Chinese civil service have generated intense controversy and little result. And even if these obstacles could be overcome, the Chinese reform leadership ought to resist the naïve assumption that a civil service really can be apolitical, especially in a one-party state.

Separation of Party and Government

This raises the question of the relationship of the Communist Party and the government. If the reformers' goal of separating the state from the economy is proving difficult to attain, perhaps the state's involvement in the economy can better serve the goal of modernization through the separation of Party and government—another frequently advanced reformist goal. According to Zhao Ziyang:

> [T]he Party exercises political leadership, which means that it formulates political principles, points the political direction, makes major policy decisions and recommends cadres for key posts in organs of state power.

The government's role is to admininster and provide leadership over practical matters, including economic affairs. Yet, Zhao also said that;

> local Party committees at the provincial, municipal and county levels should exercise political leadership in local work, . . . ensuring that the decrees of the central government are implemented. Their principal responsibilities should be . . . to ensure the implementation in their local areas of directives from governments of higher levels and from the State Council; to propose policy decisions on important local issues; . . . to co-ordinate activities of the various local organizations.[13]

Local Party officials could hardly be blamed for a certain confusion about the boundaries to which Zhao was asking them to restrict themselves, or for using his statement to stick their noses into just about anything they liked. So while Zhao complained in October 1987 about the continuing 'lack of distinction between the functions of the Party and those of the government[,] and the substitution of the Party for the government', neither his speech nor any subsequent developments have produced much progress on this front. When questioned about the division of labour between them, Party Secretary Bai Runzhang and Mayor Liu Baolu of Xinji Municipality conveyed a clear sense that the important thing was how closely and easily they worked together in planning and leading economic development, which comprised the bulk of their work.

One key element of personnel reform would be the simplification of lines of administrative authority over state officials. The system of 'dual rule' which has evolved in China since 1949 made officials responsible both to their superiors in their particular bureaucratic hierarchy (i.e. vertical [*tiaotiao*] rule) and also the Party authorities at their own level (i.e. horizontal [*kuaikuai*] rule). With two very different authorities to please, it is no wonder that state officials felt confused about what was expected of them, could not discern or pursue a clear career path, and as a result often acted passively. If the reformers seek to develop a more technocratic corps of officials by encouraging their careers, they must abolish the duality of personnel authority over them. But so far there is little indication that this has been done, or that it could be done until such time as Party and government could be separated in a meaningful way.

This is not the only contradiction relating to the separation of Party and government. At this historical juncture it is quite possible that such a separation could be somewhat self-defeating in the sense that it could damage the very reform project of which it is itself an important part. At the Seventh National People's Congress, which met in April 1988, Li Peng became premier, and Zhao Ziyang, who had held the post temporarily until then, moved over to become party secretary-general on a full-time basis. This expressed and symbolized the policy of separating the Party and the government. In early September, Zhao told an American guest that '[t]hings were different when I was premier. I do not directly deal with economic affairs . . .'[14] This was contemporaneous with a major retreat on price reform, a policy Zhao had advocated vigorously. It seems entirely plausible that Zhao's having vacated direct leadership of the government made possible this back-pedalling on economic reform. Whether this was an example of it or not, it is clear that reformers face a serious dilemma: they need control of the state to keep reform policies moving foward (especially through the periodic crises they engender), but by dividing party and government leadership they may put that control at risk.

The State in the Economy: Planner or Entrepreneur?

The major conclusion is that it has been very difficult for the reformist central leadership to translate into practice its deep desire to have the economy operate on the basis of a more purely economic rationality. It has been unable to find administrative forms either that separate middle- and local-level state organs from the economy or that keep their economic roles within tightly defined or at least controllable boundaries. As China approaches the age of forty, the state's bureaux and leaders retain a broad and deep capacity to act on and in the economy.

It is a reflection of the latitude available to them that they have inserted themselves into the economy in widely different ways. Two very different patterns have emerged from a study of the political economy of development in two counties.[15] In one, county-level state organs have taken on the role of economic entrepreneur—forming businesses, assembling venture capital, attracting junior partners, playing the market, and competing vigorously with enterprises in other localities. In the other, it has played the role of development planner and administrator, contenting itself with overseeing and elaborating the economic environment in which others—state enterprises, cooperative firms, and local businesses—can operate and compete.

The Developmental State in Xinji Municipality[16]

In Xinji, the county government concentrated on development planning. Its forte was infrastructure projects that broke bottlenecks and opened up economic terrain upon which economic agents other than itself could act. The foci of these projects changed over time with the shifting economic priorities of the Maoist and then the post-Maoist leadership. But what remained constant was its preoccupation with development planning rather than its own entrepreneurial activities. That is, it did not go into business itself, but preferred to improve the conditions for others to do so.

Some examples will highlight its activities during the late 1970s, before the reformist tide began to sweep over China. In 1978–79 it planned, put together financing for, and oversaw construction of a 5 million yuan water conservancy project in the southern third of the county, an area of endemic drainage and salinity problems. In the late 1970s it made the administrative contacts that enabled a commune lock factory, which had been producing for a very localized market, to distribute its products throughout the entire province. Its Foreign Trade Bureau put a village production brigade in touch with the provincial Native Products Company, which extended to them the credit they needed to undertake mink-raising and which acted as their purchasing agent.

As the reform period got underway, the substance of the local government's developmental work shifted somewhat—toward market development—but its concentration on development planning and its eschewal of going into business for itself did not. The centrepiece of its economic activity in the first half of the 1980s was the Hebei Number One Market, a huge shopping centre comprising an enormous office and retail block, over 350 residential/commercial condominia,[17] and row upon row of open market stalls. In this marketplace large state sector firms went cheek by jowl with small suburban and rural workshops to market a wide range of products, including the fur and leather goods that were a local specialty. The municipal government organized this market competition, but did not play in it by starting its own new companies.

Hebei Number One Market was coordinated with another major developmental activity of the municipal government: vigorous urban and environmental planning. In fact, the Market was originally motivated by the then-county government's desire to relieve the serious congestion that clogged downtown streets on market days, and thereby make the town more commodious. The Market was fronted by a brand-new divided boulevard, on the other side of which a modern new park and zoo had been constructed. The Urban Planning and Environmental Protection Bureau of the Municipal Government had formulated a complex, comprehensive master plan for the town, which involved moving entire factories to new industrial zones downwind from residential areas. The government had also completed a network of paved roads to every rural township under its jurisdiction, an achievement which had permitted one of the poorest and most remote villages to go into the fireworks business and in the space of a few years become one of the most prosperous. In agriculture, the government was engaged in fine-tuning cropping patterns through intensive research and experimentation into the comparative advantage of each village and township. It was also investing in new underground drip irrigation, an expensive and relatively new technology for which it was consulting with Israeli agronomists.

The Entrepreneurial State in Guanghan[18]

The Guanghan County Federation of Rural Supply and Marketing Cooperatives was, according to its director, an administrative rather than an economic agency, charged with coordinating and assisting its constituent village cooperatives by purchasing, warehousing and wholesaling or retailing their products. Yet in 1986 it was planning a ten-storey convention centre, including retail space, a convention hall and a hotel, in the county seat! This enterprise had little if any relationship to its administrative function. To finance this, it had taken out loans from the local banks, but had also gone directly to banks in nearby mountainous, poor counties whose narrower developmental horizons left banks there with excess liquidity to loan out at rates well below those in Guanghan. It had also syndicated a loan to local peasant investors. In addition, it had established food processing factories 'in order to make money in the face of stiff competition', to quote the Director of the Federation of Rural Supply and Marketing Cooperatives. The Guanghan Second Light Industry Bureau was establishing a new nylon conveyer belt factory, for the financing of which it had taken on its sibling agency in a poor county as a junior partner (even though that agency provided more than half the capital).

In fact, banking itself had become an entrepreneurial activity in Guanghan. Banks there had profit targets in late 1986, and were establishing specialized trust companies, both absent in Xinji. Urban construction in Guanghan took the form of investment in neon lights and snappy new storefronts that had the decided look of a little Hong Kong. Urban planning also seemed to go by the board: street markets remained crowded and noisy, as Xinji must have been before the Number One Market was built. Yet the various government bureaux clearly had at their disposal resources which they spent on themselves. The Guanghan Guest House was brand-new, and sported automated doors, a mirrored, gold-lit lobby, carpet, modern furniture, and a television and refrigerator in each room—again, reminding one much more of Hong Kong than Chengdu. It charged a nightly rate several times higher than its simple Shulu counterpart.

The major difference between these two localities is not in their level of prosperity; average per capita income was only 15 per cent higher in Guanghan. Rather it is in the way in which the state has inserted itself into the economy. The Xinji government organized, regulated and planned the economy, including the market, while in Guanghan government agencies started businesses and engaged in financial and entrepreneurial wizardry. Both localities were enjoying economic success—at least as measured by growth indicators—as well as political favour. Clearly, then, the reform programme has opened up space for the state to orient itself to the economy in a variety of ways.

Conclusion

This is probably as much if not more the result of the failures of the administrative reforms as of their successes. The reformist leadership in Beijing has undertaken several initiatives to re-orient state administration of the economy. Most have failed or at best have had very mixed results. Indeed, some parts of the reform programme contradict others. Specifically, the state's administrative apparatus has not shrunk but in fact grown considerably. Enterprise managers have not gained significant autonomy from local state officials. (Moreover, Guanghan illustrates how state officials can prove adept at becoming enterprise leaders.) Administrative reforms to put in place a taxation system to deprive local governments of financial leverage over local enterprises have been reversed. Bankruptcy, which could put enterprises at risk of dissolution, in turn causing difficulties for local governments that have to deal with the consequences, has been derailed. Banks have not been made autonomous. The state itself has been unable to separate government administration from political control generally, or more specifically to reform and depoliticize its personnel practices.

What the reform leadership has been successful at doing is opening up new opportunities and horizons for economic activity. By decentralizing economic power down to localities, and by giving its approval and encouragement to the growth of the market and entrepreneurial activities, the reform project has expanded the scope of activities in which local state leaders and administrators can properly and readily engage. But by failing to impose a new, less political form on state organization and administration in the localities, reform has left the question of the relationship of the state and the economy to be resolved by the interplay of local state officials and economic actors. Since this is not only China, with its strong statist traditions and political culture, but also state socialist China, in this interplay state actors have the upper hand over civil society in general. Moreover, because China is also large and diverse, local state actors are imprinting themselves on the economy in multifarious ways.

Two general conclusions emerge, then. If the first decade of the reform period is any guide, state socialist China will continue to be a country resistant to the imposition of authority or organizational form from the top.[19] The formal templates and the associated pronouncements of the centre will always be there, but so too will be the frustrated plaints that local officials just are not behaving. Efforts at administrative reform of the bureaucracy, management, government finance, enterprise responsibility, development finance, or personnel will continue to be stymied by locally rooted political forces and structures.

On the other hand, and contrary to the popular stereotype of local state socialist institutions and officials as resistant to change, there will be great changes. Many provincial, municipal and county officials will continue to work their will actively upon the economy. They will engage their administrative apparatus in a wide range of undertakings to promote and take advantage of economic development. But they will do so in multitudinous ways that cannot be anticipated. Many of these will be different from the plans of and will cause consternation to central reform leaders. State socialist China's mid-life crisis will, as this anthropomorphism suggests, be a period of risk, unpredictability and uncertainty. The head and the body will pull in different directions. But it will also be one capable of great vitality and creativity. The old dog of the state administration is learning new tricks daily, but not from listening to the master's voice.

1. To be consistent with conceptual usage in comparative politics, the term 'state' is used here to refer to the totality of political institutions, including

the Communist Party, the government, and the mass organizations associated with them. This differs from a common usage in comparative communist or socialist studies, in which the term 'state' refers to the government,
and is therefore differentiated from the Communist Party.

2. State Statistical Bureau, *Statistical Yearbook of China, 1986* (Oxford: Oxford
   University Press, 1986) p. 516.
3. 'Decision of the Central Committee of the Communist Party of China on
   Reform of the Economic Structure', *Beijing Review* XXVII (29 October, 1984):
   pp. i–xvi.
4. Chen Ji, of the Chinese Trade Union Federation, recently admitted that
   forty-nine strikes had occurred in the first six months of 1988. The number
   is undoubtedly higher.
5. 'AFP Views Machine Factory Wage Bonus Plan', *Foreign Broadcast Information
   Service* (hereafter *FBIS*), 30 June, 1986.
6. 'The Law of the People's Republic of China on Industrial Enterprises Owned
   by the Whole People (Adopted on 13 April, 1988 at the First Session of the
   Seventh National People's Congress)', *China Daily*, 16 May, 1988: Business
   Weekly 2–3.
7. 'Party Promotes Enterprise Law', *Beijing Review*, 23 May, 1988, p. 11.
8. Lee, *From Revolutionary Cadres to Party Technocrats* (Berkeley: University
   of California Press, forthcoming) ch. 14, p. 16.
9. 'Contract System May Be Changed', *China Daily*, 3 August, 1988:4.
10. 'Bankrupt Firm Sold at Auction', *China Daily*, 27 September, 1986; Li
    Rongxia, 'First Bankruptcy Shocks China', *Beijing Review* XXIX, 36 (8 Sep-
    tember, 1986), pp. 25–7.
11. The division of responsibility here is complex and unclear. According to
    Party Chairman Zhao Ziyang, local Party committees are to 'recommend
    cadres for key posts in local state organs'. Zhao Ziyang, 'Advance Along the
    Road of Socialism With Chinese Characteristics—Report Delivered at the
    Thirteenth National Congress of the Communist Party of China on 25
    October, 1987', *Beijing Review* XXX, 45:38.
12. Melanie Manion, 'The Cadre Management System Post-Mao: The Appoint-
    ment, Promotion, Transfer and Removal of Party and State Leaders', *China
    Quarterly* 102 (June 1985), p. 227.
13. Zhao, 'Advance', p. 38. Emphasis added.
14. Ellen Salem, 'What Price Reform?', *Far Eastern Economic Review* CXLI, 38 (22
    September, 1988), p. 70.
15. They are also not exhaustive at the levels of theory or practice. Studies of
    other localities or other periods may suggest other patterns. This study
    began in 1979 with field work in Shulu County, now known as Xinji
    Municipality, that was conducted jointly with Phyllis Andors, Stephen
    Andors, Mitch Meisner and Vivienne Shue. Subsequent field research was
    done in Xinji and in Guanghan County with Professor Shue. Several articles
    by Professor Shue and by me on topics not directly related to the present
    discussion have already appeared in print, and a book, tentatively entitled
    The Tethered Deer: The Political Economy of Shulu County, is under prep-
    aration.
16. Xinji Municipality is located approximately 70 km east of Shijiazhuang City
    (the capital of Hebei Province), to which it is connected by paved road and
    by railway. It is a rural rather than suburban area, situated well out onto
    the North China Plain. With its agriculture engaged primarily in grain
    production, it is about average for its area in rural development. But it is
    relatively advanced industrially; in fact, it is the most industrially advanced

county in the prefecture. In 1978, gross value of industrial output (GVIO) made up 55 per cent of total output value by official count, and by 1986 the figure was 63 per cent. Per-capita income was 88 yuan in 1978, well below the national average though above average for Shijiazhuang Prefecture; in 1986 it was up to 522 yuan. Still, in 1978 only 4 per cent of the county's population was classified as 'non-rural householders', and by 1986 this figure had risen only to 6 per cent. With 537 persons per km^2 and 5.4 persons per cultivated hectare in 1978, it is densely populated. It has never been a national model of economic development, either in the Maoist or post-Maoist periods.

Until 1986, the place was known as Shulu County. In May of that year, it was redesignated Xinji Municipality (after the name of the county seat) as part of a national plan to highlight rural localities with rapid rates of growth and set them apart from the surrounding counties for which it was anticipated that they would provide a centre. Its shape and composition remained unchanged, though: it still takes in the same rural districts as it did before.

17. These were two-storey units sold to households, with store fronts downstairs and apartments upstairs.

18. Guanghan County lies northeast of Chengdu, Sichuan, its county seat situated 30 km out along the major trunk roadway and railway line leading toward Xi'an. During then Provincial Secretary Zhao Ziyang's tenure in Sichuan in the earliest days of post-Maoist reform, it was selected as a keypoint for experimentation in institutional restructuring—in particular for the separation of Party leadership from government administration. Located in the fertile Chengdu Plain, it is well endowed for agriculture. With 8.7 per cent of its population classified as non-rural householders in 1985, it is slightly more urbanized than Xinji. But it is much more densely populated, with 925 people per km^2 and fifteen people per cultivated hectare. Thus it has given great emphasis to industry, which in 1985 accounted for two-thirds of gross output value. Only with these levels of industrialization could per-capita rural incomes remain at the relatively high level of 602 yuan.

19. This point is argued much more fully in Shue, *The Reach of the State: Sketches of the Chinese Body Politic* (Stanford: Stanford University Press, 1988).

3. The Long March towards Bureaucratic Rationality

OVER the past ten years China has been trying to pull off two tricks simultaneously, neither one of which, taken on its own, would be considered easy. It is trying to master the mechanics of the development process so as to bring the world's most populous country into the twentieth century before that century itself runs out. It is trying to unlearn the textbook socialism it had digested by rote from the Soviet Union in the 1950s and which, while promising security and social justice, has only succeeded in delivering these at a subsistence level and at the price of continued stagnation.

The country's growth record in the last decade has made western observers less sceptical concerning the country's development potential than they once were. Simple reform measures in the rural areas have given an impetus to agriculture that remains for a large part beyond the stifling reach of local bureaucrats. But if this replay of the Maoist strategy of starting with the countryside and surrounding the cities is proving its worth, the real challenge remains in the urban areas, the heartland of what remains of the Marxist-Leninist order, the power base of an entrenched and conservative bureaucracy. Here, China-watchers are much less sanguine that the raft of reforms initiated by the Party in October 1984 can fulfill their promise.

Not only is the bureaucracy, as in the Soviet Union, jealous of its privileges, but with every attempt at dismantling, inflation is seeping through the cracks of a structure in which the concrete had already set. Price increases for the first quarter of 1988 hit double digits in many cities and a recession now threatens Shanghai, once the jewel in the Chinese socialist crown, and at present relegated to sixth place in the provincial and municipal growth league.

Yet one could plausibly argue that economic growth can buy off some of the pain incurred in moving away from the Soviet model. Indeed, here China may have a decisive advantage over the Soviet Union where Mikhail Gorbachev is asking both worker and bureaucracy to swallow their reform medicine with little to offer in the way of economic inducement except even heavier doses of the stuff further down the road. The problem is much the same in the East European economies. China, with an average GNP growth rate estimated by the World Bank to be in excess of 9 per cent since 1980, will not find it beyond its resource to scrape up the odd yuan or two to add a touch of comfort and dignity to the retirement of elderly and recalcitrant comrades.

The China–EEC Management Programme

The China–EEC Management Programme (CEMP) offers a unique observation platform from which to track some of the recent changes in the country's industrial structure following the reforms. The CEMP is currently located in the Commission for Restructuring the Economic System, now under the leadership of the Prime Minister, Li Peng, and since 1984 it has been running a project-based Master of Business Administration course in close collaboration with eleven state-owned industrial enterprises. The students and European faculty of CEMP have thus been privileged to observe at close quarters many of the day-to-day problems and opportunities confronting Beijing-based medium-sized industrial firms as they cope with the new environment.

What follows is not a detailed description of what has been culled by the CEMP over four years but an attempted interpretation of the pattern that can be discerned as it slowly emerges out of the reform process. The pattern is impressionistic and can be read in different ways according to where one stands and what one is looking for so that the interpretation presented has the character of a working hypothesis rather than a definitive judgement.

Formalization and Decentralization

We can perhaps best understand the challenge facing China as it modernizes through a simple conceptual scheme. In the late

1960s and the early 1970s research in the field of organizational studies demonstrated pretty conclusively that the scope for decentralization within a firm is to an important extent determined by how far internal processes can be formalized, that is to say, set down on paper, standardized into a set of repetitive routines, and reduced to a set of unambiguous measures. This link between decentralization and formalization also holds good for relations between firms. If internal bureaucratic processes such as budgeting require quantifiable measures of input and output and articulated planning and control systems which feed on them, efficient external markets require well formed prices emerging from a large volume of standardized transactions conducted within a light regulatory framework.

The claim that since markets are more decentralized than bureaucracies they must therefore be more formalized, however, may raise a few eyebrows. But formalization as used here means less paperwork, not more; it expresses the ability to capture a complex reality and to reduce it to a few simple measures such as prices and volume, something that markets generally do better than bureaucracies.

More importantly for our assessment of the Chinese situation, where economic or managerial transactions cannot be formalized at all, where they cannot be set down on paper or standardized, they can only be efficiently handled on a face-to-face basis. They cannot be decentralized beyond a very small number of close subordinates who are known and trusted, without leading to ambiguity, opportunistic behaviour, and ultimately loss of control. Where decentralization is forced upon a system with a weak capacity for formalization, it quickly fragments into a collection of local fiefdoms where the exercise of personal hierarchical power asserts itself.

Before 1949 China had oscillated between periods of excessive centralization which threatened stagnation, and decentralization in which centrifugal tendencies threatened the integrity of the social fabric. The adoption of a Marxist-Leninist bureaucracy in the 1950s appeared to offer the prospects of limited decentralization without a loss of control by the centre, a move away from the fiefs of feudalism—towards greater formalization. This proved to be illusory. The lack of economic rationality for which Marxist-Leninist central planning has now become notorious, meant that a bureaucratic order could never stabilize long enough to take root. As in the case of the Soviet and East European economies, the key to survival was to find a way round the bureaucratic rule rather than to follow it, and this led to a constant process of bargaining and a personalization of relationships.

This drift back towards the fiefs was made easier by a strong cultural preference for personalized face-to-face relationships and what Talcot Parsons termed a particularistic social structure. An impersonal market order governed by abstract rules, whatever success it might have enjoyed in trading centres such as Hong Kong and Taiwan, goes against the core values of what remains for the most part a peasant society.

Under-bureaucratization

If this conceptual scheme has any validity then the western view of the current economic reforms in China as a push from bureaucratic order into a market one is fundamentally incorrect and misleading. China is attempting a decentralization towards markets from a much lower point on the formalization scale than western observers realize. The problems it faces in achieving its aims are therefore quite different to those confronting a more advanced economy such as that of the Soviet Union, also striving to reform its structure.

China's task is easier than the Soviet Union's because it has less unlearning to do. Although its bureaucracy is clad in Marxist–Leninist garb, it remains essentially patrimonial, more fluid, and thus less entrenched than the Soviet one. To be sure, plenty of resistance to the reforms can be met within the middle ranks of the bureaucracy, but in contrast to the Soviet Union where the conservatives still appear to be in the saddle, in China they are very much on the defensive and confronting a leadership cohesively aligned behind the reform.

At the same time, China's task is more difficult than the Soviet Union's because, along with other developing countries, it has a much longer road to travel before reaching a market order. In particular, it still has to build the kind of rational–legal bureaucracy that European nation-states acquired between the sixteenth and the nineteenth centuries and on which a workable

market society ultimately depends. At present it lacks both
the educated manpower and the communications infrastructure
required for this task. Contrary to popular western views, China
today does not suffer from too much bureaucracy and probably
never has; it suffers from too little.

More important perhaps, China suffers from a lack of that
peculiarly western creation: bureaucratic rationality—an ability
to devise impersonal and universal rules that are sufficiently
credible and fair to be widely accepted. Its legal and judicial
systems remain embryonic and the vague and contradictory
regulations that rain down daily on the heads of hapless enterprise managers are, of necessity, either ignored or bargained
away.

For example, the various kinds of contract responsibility systems that have been experimented with in industrial enterprises
since the early 1980s and institutionalized over the last two
years have been presented to the outside world and to Chinese
enterprise managers themselves as devices to put some distance
between their firms and the bureaucracy that supervises them.
Enterprises enter into a contract with the state under which they
will be guaranteed a certain quantity of inputs in return for a
certain quantity of outputs. Factory directors, now acting as the
representatives of their firms, become responsible for the profits
and losses incurred in transforming inputs into outputs.

The closest western equivalent to this process is Management
by Objectives (MBO) which gained popularity in the 1960s.
MBO aims to integrate the different parts of an organization's
activity whilst allowing some delegation to occur. Delegation is
a limited form of decentralization in which the power to set
objectives remains in the hands of the superior. The rationality
of MBO is coextensive with the rationality of the objectives set.
In western economies the prices and costs used in target setting
are derived from the markets external to the firm so that bureaucratic rationality builds, so to speak, on economic rationality. In
China, by contrast, the targets used in the different responsibility systems are not derived from the possibilities of the
external environment but simply from past performance—last
year's output plus 7 per cent across a whole industry—often
with little regard for variations in individual circumstances.

Bureaucratic Feudalism

Setting targets is in fact a difficult business in China. The external environment is opaque and relevant market information does not flow. Price reforms have hardly begun so that the economic signals that do get through to enterprise managers and their supervisory agencies are distorted and distrusted. The objectives set to an enterprise are thus derived solely from its past performance and largely independently of its external competitive environment. The resulting lack of realism of such targets more often than not leads to their renegotiation, a process the success of which relies on the quality of the 'relationship' that a factory director has built up with his supervisor. The enterprise once more finds itself in the hands of a supervising bureau that can exercise power even more arbitrarily than before the reforms, since then it had to operate within the constraints of a central planning system that specified output targets down to the last widget. This rigid centralized system is on the way out, but since decentralization has taken place in an environment that in most parts of China remains inhospitable to self-regulating market processes it has not effectively reached down to the enterprise level. It has, however, reached local administrations that—in the absence of a credible regulatory framework—have been able to exercise informal control over the enterprise under their care and bought them into their fiefdoms. Except in certain provinces such as Guangdong and Jiangsu which are more developed and hence 'market driven', the outcome has often been a kind of industrial 'feudalism' in which a supervising agency promises protection from environmental threats to its brood of firms in return for loyalty and obedience. The contact is a highly personalized one conducted on a face-to-face basis which escapes high level administrative control. In Eastern Bloc countries a milder form of this affliction goes by the name of the 'soft budget constraint'.

On the ground the situation is not as bleak as it has been depicted here. The country is growing rapidly and has undergone a fundamental transformation. Shops are stocked with goods that were simply unavailable four years ago and their quality is slowly improving. The analysis presented here suggests, however, that in some respects these successes are being

achieved in spite of the urban reforms rather than because of
them. Energies have been released that threaten to overwhelm
a bureaucratic apparatus designed for another age—in Marxist
parlance, the forces of production are once more running ahead
of the relations of production.

Conclusion

I have suggested that the relations of production are in urgent
need of greater formalization if we are not to witness yet another
swing of the pendulum towards the centre in an age-old cycle
of loosening-up, chaos, loss of control, and tightening up again.
But formalization, to be durable, will need a stronger foundation
of economic and bureaucratic rationality than the reforms have
been able to secure thus far. China may discover, as Japan did
a century ago, that the West has more to offer than its technology,
but that to buy 'off the shelf'—as it did with Marxist-Leninism
nearly forty years ago—may lead to rejection by the host culture.

4. Leadership and Authority in the Chinese Communist Party

TWO competing models of leadership and authority have divided the Chinese Communist Party (CCP) since 1949. Most central leaders have generally supported institutionalizing authority in party committees with 'collective leadership' as the operational mode of decision-making. Contrary to China's two-thousand year history of monarchical absolutism, such leaders as Liu Shaoqi and Deng Xiaoping looked to the establishment of an impersonal party machine with authority vested in committees, not individual leaders, as the solution to China's modern political and economic crises. Without embracing constitutional democracy, these 'orthodox Leninists' considered institutional controls on the single leader a major goal of the Chinese Communist regime, especially following the Maoist interregnum of 'patriarchal despotism' (1955–76). Although willing to employ charismatic authority in state-society relations, China's orthodox Leninists believe that within party councils all leaders should subordinate their individual will to collective deliberation and formal procedures in conformity with the gradual development of a system of impersonal, official roles.

Other leaders, in contrast, advocated a 'leader principle' for the CCP based on a radical charismatic model of authority. Contemptuous of institutional authority, they considered the CCP an instrument of the supreme leader's will, organized to aid *him* in achieving national unity and the revolutionary transformation of society. The leader's 'thought' provided the utopian vision for change, which other party leaders and cadres must 'study' as the basis for all policies and political action. Executive command, not procedural deliberation, united the party with the leader's 'heroic will', rather than the deterministic 'forces of history', driving the revolution forward. Without the Qin Shihuang-like despot to issue commands for modernizing the polity and the economy, the party and the entire country would fragment into regional and local sub-systems of power.

The heartfelt charisma of the strong leader superseded the impersonal organization in eliciting the mass loyalties and national sacrifice necessary to build a strong China.

Since 1949 the relative influence of these two diametrically opposed models have shaped the internal struggles over policy and power. During the early 1950s, the imperatives of economic planning and the construction of a modern bureaucratic apparatus along Soviet lines strengthened collective leadership in the CCP, especially after Stalin's death in March 1953. But by the late 1950s, Mao's impatience with China's moderate economic growth and increasing bureaucratization led to his personal assault on the institutional structures of decision-making formulated at the 8th Party Congress in 1956. Although the disastrous effects of the 'Great Leap Forward' (1958–60) would lead Mao to retreat temporarily to the 'second front' of decision-making, by the mid-1960s Mao exploited his 'personality cult' to mobilize Red Guards against the party machine and its top leader, Liu Shaoqi. The ten-year Cultural Revolution did, indeed, see an all-out promotion of the 'leader principle' with corresponding criticism of collective leadership principles, such as the separation of party and government, and institutional controls on the leader. Yet, following Mao's death in 1976 and the subsequent purge of the radical 'Gang of Four', the new pragmatic leadership headed by Deng Xiaoping resuscitated the collective leadership model. Since 1978, party propaganda and institutional reform have aimed at subordinating individual leaders at the central and lower levels to the organization, while regularizing internal procedures and 'democratic' practices destroyed by Mao's assault on the party apparatus. Despite some successful reform in the party's decision-making and in the leadership style of the CCP élite, however, the appeal of the 'great leader' to party cadres and population alike may remain strong—even after the death of Mao Zedong.

The Pre-1949 Legacy

The conflict between the collective leadership and charismatic models of leadership and authority in the CCP can be traced to the pre-liberation struggle for power. From 1921 to 1927 the founders of the party, especially Chen Duxiu, were profoundly affected by the anti-despotic impulses of the 1919 May Fourth movement and Lenin's 'corporate' model of the Communist Party. Monarchical authority and its residues in post-1911 China were the *primary* cause of China's political backwardness, they argued, and must, therefore, be avoided at all costs in the young Communist Party. While the Kuomintang (KMT) granted wide powers to Sun Yat-sen as the party's 'chief', communist leaders, in contrast, demonstrated their fear of excessive personal authority by vesting authority in a 'democratic committee system . . . with a secretary [Chen Duxiu] elected from the [executive] committee members to serve as a coordinator'.[1] Aware that popular admiration in China for 'a real emperor to assume authority' made the degeneration into individual dictatorship a permanent threat, even in the CCP, Chen Duxiu insisted that the 'proletarian class must maintain close watch over the revolutionary leader'. 'They cannot give him free rein', Chen warned in 1921, which is why Chen favoured a 'central collective structure' of decision-making instead of a single leader.[2] Following the near destruction of the CCP during the late 1920s, however, the new party leader, Li Lisan, adopted an autocratic leadership style while crushing all internal criticism and debate. Though Li was quickly deposed, the party leadership reiterated its commitment to collective principles and procedures, despite its fight for survival in the urban underground. 'Even though the Bolshevik style of party organization has been [recently] promoted', one document noted after Li's dismissal, 'respect for the patriarch has not completely disappeared, for there are still comrades who are not allowed to speak . . . and are not willing to risk opposing such leaders . . .'[3] The problem of excessive personal authoritarianism was, in other words, a function of *both* imperious leaders and obsequious followers.

Beginning with the 'Long March' in 1934–35, however, the imperatives of fighting a war with the KMT led CCP leaders to rely increasingly on the single leader. At the crucial 1935 Zunyi Conference, Mao Zedong was 'establish[ed] in the leading position of the Red Army and the Party Center', though other leaders, most notably the Russian returned student Zhang Wentian, retained direct control over 'the party's central daily affairs'.[4] Yet, despite the inflation of Mao's personal authority, the 6th Party Plenum in 1938 reaffirmed collective principles, such as quorum requirements for Politburo meetings and committee authority over public criticism of top leaders.[5] By 1943, Mao's personal stature was further enhanced with the creation of the Mao cult which top communist leaders, including 'orthodox Leninists' like Liu Shaoqi, supported to counterbalance Chiang Kai-shek's self-promotion as China's national leader. Mao's authority over top party policy councils was also expanded by the March 1943 decision granting the chairman authority to 'make final decisions regarding all problems discussed by the Central Secretariat'.[6] By putting Mao in charge of the Secretariat the Central Committee did not, however, violate its sovereignty and, more importantly, it still denied Mao the absolute authority over the broad policy-making powers of the Politburo. Nonetheless, by 1949, Mao Zedong had undoubtedly become the dominant political figure in the Chinese communist movement with authority that seemingly contradicted the opposition of the early May Fourth generation of CCP leaders to the powerful single leader.

The Struggle over Leadership and Authority, 1949–76

After assuming national political power, the CCP returned to its collective traditions. Mao himself criticized 'the habitual practice of one individual to monopolize the conduct of affairs and decide important problems', while insisting that 'a sound system of Party committee meetings . . . be instituted in all *leading bodies*' with the authority to review '[a]ll important problems . . . for discussion. . . .'[7] Mao also seemingly denigrated his own cult by forbidding the celebration of party leaders' birthdays and honouring places, streets, and enterprises with their names.[8] Although public pronunciamentos still described Mao as 'the great leader whom the Chinese people need and the helmsman on whom they can rely', the post-1949 leadership structure in the CCP and the rapid growth of the state structure reduced the Chairman's room for manoeuvre, especially after the inauguration of a central economic planning apparatus in 1953. Intellectuals, too, apparently voiced opposition to leader cults as questions arose over whether chanting 'Long Live Chairman Mao' constituted the same kind of irrational hero worship promoted by Chiang Kai-shek during the war.[9] '"History is not made by Chairman Mao" and "Mao did not personally win battles" so why do we shout "Long Live"?', one intellectual ruefully inquired. Although the public cult persisted throughout the early 1950s, even Mao generally accepted the necessity of collegial deliberation in China's early years of economic reconstruction, though he did apparently force the leadership to accept his views on China's entry into the Korean War (1950–53).

Beginning in 1955, however, the Chairman showed growing impatience with his top colleagues on basic issues of economic policy, especially in agriculture, which led to an increasingly arrogant and interventionist leadership style that continued until his death in 1976. The critical watershed probably came on 31 July 1955 when Mao, ignoring the decisions on economic planning and agricultural collectivization hammered out in top party and state policy-making bodies such as the broadly representative National People's Congress, personally pushed for a rapid speed-up in the formation of rural collectives in a speech to provincial and other low-level party secretaries. Despite warnings from economic conservatives, such as Chen Yun, on the 'tense situation' created by inadequate grain supplies, Mao threw caution to the wind by advocating a 'socialist mass movement' in the countryside.[10] Severe problems in implementing rapid cooperativization ultimately led to temporary slowdowns, however, while Mao was undoubtedly weakened by Khrushchev's 1956 assault on Stalin. Meeting for the first time in eleven years, the Party Congress in 1956 thus decided to eliminate references to 'Mao Zedong Thought' from the party constitution and check the Chairman's personal authority with the creation of four vice-chairmanships and the Secretariat. Yet, despite such strictures, Mao still presided over the full collectivization of Chinese agriculture with his personal authority, especially in popular eyes, apparently intact. When confronted with high-level opposition to his plan to allow open debate and criticism among China's intellectuals in 1957, Mao showed complete contempt for collective decision-making procedures by personally ordering the 'Hundred Flowers' movement. Responding to one intellectual's comment in March 1957 that 'we hope the Central Committee . . . [can issue] directives to the Party committees . . . [for] only thus [can] this policy be implemented', Mao demanded: 'Don't wait till the Third Plenum; you relay and implement [the results of this conference] as soon as you return.'[11] One year later when pushing for the 'Great Leap Forward', Mao once again circumvented central leaders by ordering the formation of rural communes before formal Politburo approval while introducing key policy packages at state, not party, conferences. The pursuit of irrational utopianism in the 'Great Leap' was, indeed, a testament to the enormous persuasive powers of the chairman in a political system which, unlike the traditional Chinese bureaucracy, lacked the institutional safeguards against an errant leader.

The failure of the 'Great Leap Forward' had a dramatic impact, however, on Mao Zedong and the conflict over leadership and authority in the CCP. Following Mao's retreat to the 'second front' of policy-making in spring 1959, many central party leaders tried to reinstitute the party model outlined at the 8th Congress. From late 1959 through the mid-1960s, party propaganda reaffirmed basic principles of 'collective leadership', just as increasingly sharp and explicit attacks on Mao's personal authority were voiced in party councils and even the press. Although Mao successfully executed the purge of his major nemesis, Peng Dehuai—whose 1959 'Letter of Opinion' criticized, at least elliptically, Mao's 'Great Leap Forward' leadership style by condemning 'the growing tendency towards boasting and exaggeration' and 'a lack of realistic thinking'—the press and even Mao's own comments openly criticized 'one-man tyranny' in the party.[12] Contrary to Mao's blatant disregard for party procedure in pushing through 'Great Leap Forward' policy, the chairman now insisted that '[a]ll important matters must be discussed collectively, different opinions must be listened to seriously, and the complexities of the situation . . . must be analysed'.[13] But not all party leaders and commentary accepted this line of argument. For avid defenders of charismatic authority, such as Kang Sheng and Chen Boda, the post-'Great Leap Forward' agricultural crisis created an even greater need for 'the Party [to] have a leader of its own' with the 'revolutionary will and heroism' to overcome China's backwardness.[14] Switching his concerns from the 'thoughtless leadership' of the 'Great Leap Forward' to the leadership vacuum which characterized the CCP of the early 1960s, Mao decided to put such views to the test, especially after party leaders apparently rebuffed his 1964 call for yet another 'Great Leap Forward'.[15]

The Great Proletarian Cultural Revolution (1966–76) saw the struggle over leadership and authority divide the CCP with conflict spilling over into the streets and the general populace. Confronting an increasingly resistant central party apparatus— which forced Mao to seek political support in Shanghai—and public satire of his persona in such devastating newspaper columns as Deng Tuo's and Liao Mosha's *Three Family Village* and *Night Talks at Yanshan*, Mao launched an all-out assault on the party apparatus, beginning with the Beijing Party Committee.[16] Exploiting the long-term indoctrination of youth into the Mao cult, the chairman mobilized Red Guards, exhorting them to 'pay attention to state affairs', to bring down such longtime advocates of 'collective leadership' as Liu Shaoqi, Deng Xiaoping, and Peng Zhen.

In the heat of political battles which nearly destroyed the CCP apparatus, the personality cult reached fanatic proportions as Red Guards invoked Mao's name, committing wanton acts of violence against intellectuals, teachers, and old party cadres. 'We will fight to the death to defend Chairman Mao' became the rallying cry for what turned into a glorification of violence and power equalling the orgies of Hitler's Brown Shirts. Just as Mao's absolute authority was reaffirmed *ad nauseam*—'the party's line, principles, and policies [are] formulated *personally* by Chairman Mao', the *People's Daily* clamoured day after day— earlier proponents of collective leadership principles, such as then Guangdong Party Secretary, Zhao Ziyang, were lambasted in the press and public struggle sessions.[17]

Although the failure of new political structures, namely the Revolutionary Committees, to take hold led to a renewed 'Party rebuilding' effort during the late 1960s, Mao's personal domination of the CCP was still beyond question: '"The Party must have . . . its great leader"', the *People's Daily* insisted in quoting Lenin, otherwise the 'dictatorship of the proletariat . . . will become empty words.'[18] Following the ill-fated coup attempt by Lin Biao in 1971, Mao's personal stature apparently suffered serious deflation in popular eyes, even among the peasantry who reportedly 'criticized Mao publicly'. Yet even as his health and virtual capacity to speak declined, Mao's control of China's political scene remained intact. With his death in 1976 some Chinese could only lament that 'the revolution was now lost'.[19] But just to make sure Mao's enormous legacy was not forgotten, his radical allies, particularly Jiang Qing, ordered, contrary to Mao's own last will and testament, the construction of a mausoleum where to this day Chinese visitors pay respects to the preserved corpse of their 'great leader'.

The Transformation of Leadership and Authority, 1978–88

The rise to power of Deng Xiaoping and his pragmatic faction two years after Mao Zedong's death in 1976 had profound effects on the issue of leadership and authority in the CCP. Although less dramatic than the economic reform proposals inaugurated at the watershed 1978 3rd Party Plenum, the internal reform of the CCP's leadership structure at the central and local levels marked a radical departure from the personalistic rule of Mao Zedong. Reacting to the earlier attempt by Mao's designated successor, Hua Guofeng, to mimic the Mao cult, the new leadership outlawed leader cults and prohibited the issuing of personal 'directives' in the CCP.[20] Even CCP meeting places were ordered by the Party Propaganda Department to avoid 'hanging pictures of current leaders', while Mao's picture should, according to the same injunction, be exhibited 'sparingly' and in a 'solemn fashion in line with international standards of good appearance'.[21]

In great contrast to the Maoist style, the new leaders, including Deng Xiaoping and Zhao Ziyang, have assumed a generally low public profile, avoiding the self-promotional, celebratory politics which produced the 'blind worship of leaders' during the Cultural Revolution. Twenty years after Mao Zedong whipped up the Red Guards to a political frenzy from atop, most ironically, the Gate of Heavenly Peace, China's new leaders rarely appear in public, even during National Day celebrations on 1 October, which in recent years have seen the political content reduced in favour of a carnival-like, family-oriented event.

More importantly, Deng has outlawed the various 'campaigns' which quickly degenerated into political witch-hunts and paroxysms of violence, paralysing the party apparatus and, thereby, enhancing the leader's authority. Throughout the 1980s, leaders have, instead, been demystified and humanized in China; Zhao Ziyang's and Premier Li Peng's public personae are of competent businessmen, while Deng Xiaoping's is of a kindly grandfather who enjoys the company of his grand-children while they all watch Mickey Mouse on television.

While the Mao mausoleum, though frequently closed 'for repairs', remains a testament to the previous era of leader worship, elsewhere Mao's legacy is being gradually erased by the dismantling of statues around the country, such as the giant one at Beijing University, recently removed to make room for libraries and classrooms. In the post-1978 CCP historiography, Mao's profile has been similarly lowered. The Chinese com-munist revolution succeeded, it is now argued, not just because of the 'heroic' actions of Mao or the 'genius' of his thought, but by virtue of the 'collective' contributions of many leaders whose own 'heroic' careers are documented in the voluminous memoir literature recently published. 'Mao Zedong Thought' itself is now considered a product of the top leadership's 'collective' wisdom, while Mao's personal legacy was subjected to an 'objec-tive' analysis in 1981 that, despite protestations from lower-level cadres, condemned the 'smug' and 'arrogant' leadership style of his later years and personally blamed him, not just the radical 'Gang of Four', for the Cultural Revolution.[22]

Institutional reforms have also been introduced into the CCP to restrict the personal authority of individual leaders and expand decision-making power in the party and government. Abiding by the principle that 'individual party members are subordinate to the party organization', pragmatic party leaders, including relatively 'conservative' ones, such as Chen Yun, threw their support behind various institutional restrictions on personal authority. The post of Chairman of the CCP has been abolished and replaced by the more innocuous position of General Secretary, who is empowered to convene, but not necessarily chair, Politburo and Standing Committee meet-ings.[23] More important, perhaps, is the prohibition against one person holding the top party and government posts, thereby preventing the enormous concentration of power over the party-state apparatus which Mao wielded in the 1950s. In general, the holding of concurrent posts by individual leaders has been eliminated at all organizational levels, resurrecting practices from the pre-1949 period. Reflecting the principles embodied in the 8th Party Congress—which since 1978 has been hailed as a model—party congresses and plenums are, once again, required periodically, while lifetime tenure has been formally abolished for all party leaders.[24] To avoid a single leader's manipulation of key policy-making councils, including the Central Committee, party rules now stipulate that decisions should be taken by majority vote, while intra-party elections permit candidate lists to exceed the number of posts to be filled—a procedure that allowed delegates to the 13th Party Congress in 1987 to oust the conservative ideologue, Deng Liqun, from the Central Committee. Greater emphasis has also been given to the sovereignty of the party constitution and state law which party cadres are required to obey under the threat of punishment by state courts as well as conventional intra-party discipline. In the most potentially radical reorganization of power in China, Zhao Ziyang announced in his 13th Party Congress report a plan to dismantle the powerful 'party groups' which subject all government, education, and military bodies to the control of a few central leaders.[25] The separation of party and government—which the elimination of party groups will effectively institute—is, indeed, considered a major structural prerequisite to the erosion of individual authority in Chinese politics.

The impact of these formal changes is, of course, difficult to gauge. Even after his 'retirement' from most central posts in 1987, Deng Xiaoping's continuing personal influence on Chinese politics is substantial, though Deng reportedly delegates work on many issues to subordinates in a fashion staunchly resisted by Mao. Criticisms of Hu Yaobang for violating 'collective leadership' during his tenure as General Secretary, though possibly apocryphal, also indicate that the principle has become a central core of the post-Mao political line. And while the public may yearn for the 'decisive' actions of the single leader, especially to deal with such recent problems as inflation and corruption, the leadership seems genuinely committed to the consensus-building style which, despite its cumbersome nature, ensures more 'rational' policies. During the Mao years, basic policies were often determined by the chairman's penchant for epigrammatic remarks, such as 'take grain as the key link'—a slogan which produced a virtual agricultural disaster when implemented in regions, like Tibet, unsuitable for grain production. But since 1978, the leadership has made a conscious effort to base policies on thorough research and analysis as provided by the many 'think tanks' which have been established in Beijing, sponsored by top leaders like Zhao Ziyang and Li Peng. That the post-1978 leadership seems to have avoided potential policy disasters, such as the Yangtze River Three Gorges Project, is, indeed, a testament to this more deliberative policy-making process.

Reflecting a commitment to the separation of party and government, the revitalized National People's Congress—moribund during the Cultural Revolution—has also assumed a new role, with periodic open debate and even a recent decision to postpone a draft bankruptcy law pushed by the party. Although some economic reformers resented this action, others praised the NPC: 'For the first time in forty years', a member of the Political Restructuring Commission commented to this author, 'a non-party body has defied the Communist Party'. On vital issues Deng Xiaoping probably can still get his way. But given the combination of self-restraint on Deng's part and the enormous complexities of decisions confronting the leadership as it tackles the intricacies of reform, one leader's total domination of the Chinese political scene seems passed.

Similar changes in the 'leadership system' have been effected below the central level. During the 1950s Mao was able to circumvent the central apparatus by drawing crucial political support from provincial and lower-level leaders who often modelled their own leadership on the chairman's 'patriarchal' style. By the mid-1960s, Mao's influence among the lower ranks apparently waned, especially on the issue of agriculture, which made these leaders prime targets for the Red Guards. Yet as practitioners of a Mao-like autocracy over their own local bailiwicks, many of these leaders—the so-called 'little Maos'—were destined for criticism and removal after 1978. Just as central leaders supportive of the Maoist style, such as Wang Dongxing and his 'whatever' faction, were purged after the chairman's death, Deng and others engineered the removal of many provincial leaders opposed to the post-1978 political and economic reforms.[26]

More importantly, changes similar to those instituted at the centre have been introduced at all organizational levels, specifically to control the 'local despots' who obstruct collegial deliberation and often disobey central orders. The authority of the all-important First Party Secretary has, like that of the CCP's General Secretary, been restricted. While prohibited from holding concurrent posts in the government, party secretaries, at least at the prefecture and county levels, are now appointed for a six-year 'term' with concomitant controls on their authority to convene meetings and make personal policy decisions.[27] Though the Chinese have apparently not gone as far as the Communist Party of the Soviet Union in instituting internal party elections, still, with the separation of party and government at the local levels, the previously awesome authority of the CCP First Secretary has weakened considerably, especially over agriculture and education.

Less authority is also exercised by the local party leader in the crucial area of cadre recruitment and management where the power of appointment of government staff has been shifted to the Ministry of Personnel—a change which will undoubtedly snowball if Zhao Ziyang's recent proposals for instituting a 'national civil service' are implemented. Government officials in the past apparently had to 'guess what the ideas of the top leaders were in order to comply with their prejudices'. But under the newly proposed reforms, it is hoped that 'rule by law [will] replace rule by men', while 'efficiency and successful work' will supplant obsequious submission to authority, as the criteria for advancement.[28] Local party leaders, like their central counterparts, have been exposed to heavy doses of re-education and retraining through the revitalized Party Schools where 'leadership studies' stress 'scientific' decision-making based on analysis and the input of experts.[29] Whereas leaders were previously judged on the highly subjective basis of ideological purity and absolute loyalty to the chairman, now they are periodically evaluated according to competence and concrete achievements that, if deficient, can lead to their removal.

The 'collective leadership' model, despite official backing, is, however, still far from full realization. By the central leadership's and Deng Xiaoping's own admission, many party units throughout the country are still plagued by the 'patriarchal system'.[30] In part, this reflects the legacy of the past: twenty years of Maoist despotism left an indelible mark on the CCP that cannot be erased in the short term. For the millions of members who joined the party during the Cultural Revolution and have not yet been purged, the Maoist style of strong leadership still has great appeal, especially as the economic reforms confront growing problems that may some day require the decisive action which 'collective leadership' seems unable to provide. That Deng and other top leaders have themselves relied on irregular procedures to execute major decisions, such as the dismissal of Hu Yaobang as General Secretary by the Standing Committee rather than the Central Committee, also makes a mockery of institutional authority, 'legalization', and the 'sovereignty' of the party constitution.

Although the post-1978 period has witnessed greater adherence to constitutional prescriptions to convene congresses and plenums at periodic intervals, Deng has resorted to invoking his personal authority to push through reforms resisted by lower levels. According to reports to a November 1987 forum on 'political reform', the 'study of Deng Xiaoping thought' is the prerequisite for 'transforming the system'.[31] 'We must use Deng Xiaoping thought to unite the entire party's thought', one report noted in a style reminiscent of the Maoist days, for by 'studying and researching Deng Xiaoping's political thought on restructuring . . . all comrades will then support political reform'. To be sure, the same forum wholeheartedly denounced the blind worship of leaders noting how during the Cultural Revolution 'people really believed that only with a great leader could China avoid danger and suffering'—a situation which has fundamentally changed, it is claimed, as the populace now purportedly realizes that 'leadership of society depends heavily on well-trained leaders who take a long term view'.[32] Yet the fact that Deng, confronted with increased resistance from below, has had to resort to personalizing the reforms which aim, contrarily, at *depersonalizing* leadership and authority through institutionalization, indicates the severe dilemmas posed by the reform process in a society which evidently still responds to heartfelt charisma over impersonal organization, especially in rural areas. 'Traditionally, the Chinese people have believed that the quality of politics did not depend on political institutions', Yan Jiaqi commented in his contribution to the 1987 political reform forum, 'rather on the emperor and his ministers, but especially the emperor'. In this sense, nothing has really changed since the 1919 May Fourth Movement: Chinese culture is still considered the major obstacle to the reform of leadership and political authority.

Recent economic and social developments have also hindered the fundamental reform of leadership. In the midst of rampant inflation and increasing corruption—which the 'business-like' leaders of Zhao Ziyang and Li Peng seem unable to control—the appeal of procedural rationality and faceless 'collective leadership' is undoubtedly weakened. 'What China needs today', one high-level party intellectual told this author, 'is a *strong* liberal leader'.[33] The apparent popularity in China of Soviet leader Mikhail Gorbachev is indicative of the kind of decisive personal authority Chinese yearn for to discipline society while also saving the reforms. The more the social order degenerates because of uncontrolled corruption, the more likely it is that a leader opposed to all reforms may gain support by exploiting popular discontent, especially if Deng dies soon.

China's current leaders may, like Gorbachev, have to reverse the recent dispersal of authority at the centre, instead concentrating power to ensure the full implementation of their programme. In the tradition of eighteenth-century European 'enlightened despots' and China's own Guangxu emperor in the late nineteenth-century 'Hundred Days of Reform', fundamental transformations in society and economy may require reliance on traditional political forms—specifically despotism—to be effected. Although party intellectuals and even top leaders argue that further economic reform requires political reform, the opposite may actually be the case. Power may have to be 'over-concentrated', albeit in reformist hands, to break the bureaucratic and political bottlenecks inhibiting, and, indeed, sabotaging, economic liberalization. As long as politically powerful individuals can throw wrenches into the economy, intensifying inflation through excessive capital construction and the goods' shortages which produce it, the reform will be constantly derailed, as recently occurred in the October 1988 reimposition of central price controls. Rather than concentrating on restricting the central leader's authority and prohibiting leadership cults, perhaps Deng Xiaoping should encourage a 'liberal authoritarianism' to sweep away entrenched opponents of reform. Although this may require extensive purges and the kind of political bloodletting the post-1978 pragmatic leadership has generally avoided—witness the relatively mild party 'rectification' in 1983–85—economic events, such as the recent spectre of starvation in large areas of rural China, may dictate bold action from the centre. Forty years after liberation and more than six decades after Chen Duxiu vowed to avoid 'patriarchal' leadership in the CCP, the pendulum seems to be swinging once again in favour of a strong leader. The big question is whether he will be pro- or anti-reform.

On the other hand, perhaps China has already changed so fundamentally that another 'great helmsman', even in liberal pro-reform garb, cannot emerge with broad popular support. The penetration of commercial relationships deep into the economy and the popular psyche; the introduction of legal systems and the legal profession; the diffusion of scientific knowledge, computers, admiration for western democracies, and the irreverent attitudes displayed in popular theatre such as Peter Schaffer's play *Amadeus* (which has run in Beijing for over two years); plus the cynical reaction among all social classes to Mao Zedong's duplicity in the Cultural Revolution: all these may have immunized China against the popularization of another 'leader principle'. Despite the spectre of social 'chaos' brought on by the rapid changes created by reform, China's experiences in the Cultural Revolution may, as with Germany after the Second World War, have taught the country the horrible lessons of 'blind worship'. During the 1950s and 1960s, the Chinese 'people did not first ask: "Is this conclusion in keeping with reality"', Wang Ruoshui has argued, but 'instead, the first question they used to ask was: "Who said this?"'[34] Today, the Chinese, perhaps, are more concerned with truth than authority and may believe, in the immortal words of Tina Turner: 'We Don't Need Another Hero'.

1. Chang Kuo-t'ao, *The Rise of the Chinese Communist Party, 1921–1927, Vol. I* (Lawrence, Kansas: The University Press of Kansas, 1971), pp. 102 and 142.
2. Chen Duxiu, 'Women yao Zenmeyang Gan Shehui Geming?' (How Should We Promote the Social Revolution?), *Gongchandang* (*The Communist*) no. 5, 7 June, 1921 and 'Zhonggong Zhongyang Zhiweihui Shuji Chen Duxiu gei Gongchan Guojide Baogao' (Report to the Communist Internationale by Central Executive Secretary, Chen Duxiu), in *Zhonggong Zhongyang*

Zhengzhi Baogao Xuanji: 1922–1926) (*Collection of Central Party Political Reports*), (Zhonggong Zhongyang Dangxiao Chubanshe, 1980), p. 7.

3. Ha Cong (pseudonym), 'Chedi Shenru Wuqingde Liangtiao Luxiande Douzheng' (Thoroughly Enter into a Ruthless Two-Line Struggle), *Douzheng yu Xuexi* (*Struggle and Study*), Shaanxi Provincial Party Committee, no. 4, 14 October, 1932, p. 7.

4. Qin Yizhen, 'Zhongguo Gongchan Dang Chengli Yilaide Zhongyao Huiyi Jianjie [Lianzai yi]' (Brief Description of Important Meetings Since the Establishment of the Chinese Communist Party [Serialized, no. 1]), in *Lilun Tansuo* (*Theoretical Explorations*), Shaanxi Party School, no. 2, 1980, and Wang Jianying, (ed.), *Zhongguo Gongchan Dang Zuzhi Shi Ziliao Huibian* (*Compilation of Historical Documents on the Chinese Communist Party Organization*), (Hongqi Chubanshe, 1981) p. 234.

5. 'Kuodade Zhongyang Diliuci Quanhui Guanyu Geji Dangbu Gongzuo Guize yu Jilude Jueding' (Decision of the Enlarged Sixth Plenum on the Work Principles and Discipline of Party Units), 6 November, 1938, in *Zhongguo Gonchang Dang Fagui Zhidu Wenjian Xuanbian* (*Documentary Collection of Chinese Communist Party Regulations*) (Zhongyang Dangxiao Dangjian Jiaoyanshi, 1988), pp. 6–8. The Sixth Plenum also established Mao as the 'head' (*shou*) of the Politburo, though he was not given the same broad powers which he exercised over the Secretariat.

6. Song Yifeng, 'Zhongguo Gongchan Dang Chengli . . . [Serialized no. 3]', *Lilun Tansuo*, no. 3, 1980.

7. Emphasis added. Mao Zedong, 'On Strengthening the Party Committee System', 20 September, 1948, drafted by Mao for the Central Committee, *Selected Works of Mao Tse-Tung, Vol. IV* (Beijing: Foreign Language Press, 1969), p. 267.

8. Mao Zedong, 'Methods of Work of Party Committees', 13 March, 1949, in *Selected Works, IV*, p. 380.

9. Ai Mu, (pseudonym?), 'Mao Zhuxi Wansui' (Long Live Chairman Mao), *Xuexi* (*Study*), Vol. I, no. 4, 15 December, 1949. The author of this article defends adulation of Mao, but only after indicating strong reservations among intellectuals.

10. *Renmin Ribao* (*People's Daily*), 17 September, 1955 and 22 July, 1955, respectively.

11. Mao Zedong, 'A Talk With the Literature and Art Circle', 8 March, 1957, in Roderick MacFarquhar (ed.), *The Secret Speeches of Mao Zedong* (Cambridge, Mass.: Harvard East Asian Monograph Series, forthcoming).

12. *The Case of P'eng Teh-huai, 1959–68* (Hong Kong, Union Research Institute, 1968), p. 10.

13. Mao Zedong, 'Talk at an Enlarged Central Work Conference', 30 January, 1962, in Stuart R. Schram (ed.), *Chairman Mao Talks to the People. Talks and Letters: 1945–1971* (New York: Pantheon Books, 1974), p. 165.

14. *Hongqi* (*Red Flag*), no. 19, 1 October, 1959, and 'Reply to Letter-to-the-Editor', *Nanfang Ribao* (*Southern Daily*), 10 June, 1962.

15. Mao Zedong, 'China's Great Leap Forward', December 1964, in Schram, *op. cit.*, p. 231.

16. See, especially, Deng Tuo, 'Wang Dao he Ba Dao' (The Kingly Way and the Tyrannical Way), *Beijing Wanbao* (*Beijing Evening News*), 25 February, 1962, translated in Timothy Cheek, (guest ed.), *Chinese Law and Government*, (Armonk, New York: M. E. Sharpe Inc.), Winter 1983–84, pp. 64–5.

17. Emphasis added. *Renmin Ribao*, 1 July, 1969 and *Hongqi Ruhua* (*Red Flag*

Unfurled Like a Picture Scroll), no. 1, January 1968 (*Survey of China Mainland Press*, no. 4112, p. 2).

18. *Renmin Ribao*, 30 January, 1969. The 1969 9th Party Constitution failed, unlike its predecessors, to even mention 'collective leadership'.

19. First quote from Guangdong Light Industrial Worker, interviewed in Hong Kong by the late Sidney Liu. Second quote from worker interviewed by this author, Beijing, Summer, 1988.

20. Twelfth *Constitution of the Communist Party of China*, adopted September 1982, in *Xinhua*, 8 September, 1982.

21. *Zhibu Shenghuo* ([*Party*] *Branch Life*), Guangxi Province Edition, October 1981, p. 19.

22. Older local cadres were quoted as being 'furious that anyone dare criticize Chairman Mao'. *Zhibu Shenghuo*, December 1981, p. 5, and 'Text of CCPCC Resolution on Historical Questions', *Xinhua* 30 June, 1981, *Foreign Broadcast Information Service*, 1 July, 1981, p. K14.

23. Hu Qiaomu, 'Some Questions Concerning Revision of the Party Constitution', *Beijing Review*, no. 39, 1982, p. 17.

24. Party Congresses are required every five years and plenary sessions at least once a year. See Articles 20 and 37 of the Twelfth Party Constitution.

25. Zhao Ziyang, 'Advance Along the Road of Socialism With Chinese Characteristics', Report delivered at the 13th National Congress of the Communist Party of China, 25 October, 1987, in *Beijing Review*, 9–15 November, 1987, p. 38.

26. 'Whatever policies Chairman Mao had decided, we shall resolutely defend; whatever instructions he issued, we shall steadfastly obey', was the purported slogan of Wang's group. Eight First Party Secretaries were removed in 1978, and generally replaced by Deng supporters. Parris Chang, 'Deng's Quest for Power and Reforms: Will the Deng-Hu Setup Last?', unpublished paper, p. 7, and David S. G. Goodman, 'Changes in Leadership Personnel after September 1976', in Jürgen Domes, *Chinese Politics After Mao* (Berkeley: University of California Press, 1979), p. 43.

27. Yan Jiaqi, 'Guanyu "Dang Zheng Fenkai" he "Guojia Gongwuyuan Zhidu" Wenti' (On the Problems of the 'Separation of Party and Government' and the 'National Civil Service System'), in Wang Zhongtian *et al.*, *Deng Xiaoping Zhengzhi Tizhi Gaige Sixiang* (*Deng Xiaoping's Thought on Political Reform, Vol. I*), Central Party School, November 1987, p. 15.

28. *Interview*, Zouping county, Shandong, Summer, 1988. Courtesy Professor Michel Oksenberg, University of Michigan.

29. *Interview*, Beijing City Party Committee School, Winter, 1986.

30. *Guangming Ribao* (*Enlightenment Daily*), 19 July, 1986, (*Joint Publications Research Service*), 26 November, 1986, p. 32.

31. 'Renzhen Yanjiu Deng Xiaoping Zhengzhi Tizhi Gaige Sixiang, Shenke Linghui Dangde Shida Jingshen' (Earnestly Research Deng Xiaoping's Thought on Political Restructuring, Profoundly Understand the Great Spirit of the Party), in Wang Zhongtian, op. cit., p. 1.

32. Yan Jiaqi, op. cit., p. 9.

33. Emphasis added. *Interview*, Su Shaozhi, Beijing, Winter, 1986.

34. Wang Ruoshui, 'The Personality Cult and Ideological Alienation (Second and Last Part)', *Ching Pao*, no. 5, 10 May, 1988, p. 42.

5. The Challenge to the Social Fabric

ANITA CHAN

IN June 1988, about two weeks after the Chinese government had withdrawn subsidies for four main food items in the cities so as to divert more money to the peasants, causing price rises of 30 to 60 per cent overnight,[1] Deng Xiaoping made a surprising statement to a group of foreign guests. He said that as the government began to tackle the thorny issue of price and wage reforms the Chinese economic reforms had arrived at a 'critical stage . . . Our work must rest on facing big risks and preparing countermeasures so that the "sky won't fall down" . . .'[2] Deng did not elaborate further on what he meant by 'risks'. But it is not every day that China's top leaders so forthrightly and publicly reveal their inner worries. There was a shade of wavering confidence, yet doggedness. Deng seemed to be saying: we have reached a stage of no return; come what may, we have to steamroll ahead with the reforms. Such is the uncertain state of China's much touted 'Second Revolution'.

On the same day, student unrest broke out on the campus of Beijing University in protest against a whole range of problems, from the crisis in the educational system to corruption within the Party. Unlike the student upheaval of 1986–87, this one did not spread and was quickly quelled. But it signalled one of the many 'risks' the Chinese leaders have to be prepared to face in the coming months and years, as the new price and wage reforms begin to affect every corner of China's economy and society.

The critical nature of the problems is not readily discernible, though, in China's mass media. Ever since the reform faction of the Party élite gained a decided upper hand over the 'conservatives' at the 13th Party Congress in October 1987, the press has devoted itself to reporting on the achievements and ideological justifications of the new policies. Fortunately, a month's sojourn during the spring of 1988 in Kunming, the capital of Yunnan province, helps redress this imbalance. In the pages that follow, first-hand observations and conversations with people from all walks of life supplement China's published data.

Currents of Dissatisfaction

Today Chinese cities, especially those along the eastern sea-board, are bustling centres of economic vitality. This is borne out by the impressive statistical figures since 1978 (the year Deng Xiaoping took over the reins of power), showing sharply rising increases in national manufacturing output, in total area of floor space built, in consumer goods production, in the amount of pork consumed, and so on. Material improvements have been accompanied by a revival of some forms of cultural activities and mass entertainment: from Beijing opera to *avant garde* theatre, while on television the range is from French language-learning programmes to serialized Hong Kong *kung-fu* movies. The authorities no longer bombard the populace with political messages. Political study sessions, which used to be dreaded times for criticisms and self-criticisms, are now public arenas for airing grievances. In Kunming, not one portrait of a political leader, living or dead, was visible at the hotel that houses high-level officials on visits from Beijing. Primary school students in physical exercise classes swung their hips to the thumping beat of jazz rock rather than marching to a revolutionary cadence.

The sharp swing away from the nativistic Maoism of past decades is graphically evident everywhere. A year ago, the authorities at Beijing University, China's Oxford, unceremoniously blasted away with explosives the collosal concrete statue of Mao which had presided larger-than-life over the campus. A survey carried out in a Beijing secondary school reveals an astounding fact: only 22 per cent of the students knew who Mao Zedong was, almost none knew who Liu Shaoqi was, and only a few had heard of Zhou Enlai.[3] The Communist Party and parents alike are eager to leave the youngest generations ignorant of several decades of history. Today, a dozen years after Mao's death, after several political springs and winters, the political milieu is decidedly more relaxed; social and personal liberalization has come far. China is fast becoming depoliticized, modernized and westernized.

Given the enforced conformity and repression of the Maoist era, these changes are encouraging. A logical assumption would be that the Chinese people today should be increasingly, if not completely, satisfied with life. This very picture, in fact, had been painted for a number of years by western journalists and by some western China experts. Yet according to an opinion poll carried out in forty Chinese cities, only 60 per cent said their lives had improved since 1978. Had the poll asked whether people's lives had improved since 1985, not 1978, the percentage of affirmative responses very likely would have dropped dramatically. My interviews in Kunming indicate that the reforms had begun turning sour in people's minds by the mid-1980s. It was then that the new economic policies had begun to take root and that the new patterns of social stratification took more visible shape.

When Deng Xiaoping first returned to power, much of the populace had held high hopes for the promised reforms. The most dramatic success was a quick increase in agricultural output. Up until the mid-1980s, improved opportunities seemed to be opening for all. The pie was to become bigger and everyone was promised an equal opportunity to acquire a fair share. Now, such hopes are giving way to frustration.

Unrealistic expectations are partly to blame; and the Party's own propaganda and slogans are responsible for creating and fuelling them. Glowing figures on national production only point up one's own meagre income. Lavish praise heaped on the '10,000 yuan households' and the 'capable entrepreneurs', holding them up as national models to be emulated, only breeds frustration and jealousy. Beating the drums for people to 'look forward' infuses impatience that the promised land is still not in sight.

These unrealistic expectations are coupled to complaints about equity. Within the past few years, it has become obvious to most of the populace that a bigger pie does not always mean a bigger share, less still a fairer share. The identities of the real winners and losers in the new system are not always apparent to people, however. Very often their envy is pointed toward the wrong groups.

Winners and Losers in the Process of Social Restructuring and Restratification

Almost invariably, when asked who are doing well today under the reforms, urban people will tell you with an unmistakable tone of resentment that they are the 'private households' (*getihu*), plus the workers in profitable collective enterprises, plus the peasants. But these are misplaced targets of frustration.

The Scapegoats of Frustration

The 'private households' are the self-employed repairmen, the street hawkers selling breakfast pancakes or smuggled imported clothing, the taxi drivers who own their own cabs, the family-operated noodle shop owners. The average income of these small-time entrepreneurs comes to 3,000 to 4,000 yuan a year, one to two times more than the average national urban income of 1,400 yuan. But what the complainants do not take into account is that these 'private households' do not enjoy any social benefits, or housing, or workplace subsidies, or labour insurance, or medical care, or pensions, and that their incomes are erratic and the survival of their business precarious, not to mention the long working hours and often unpleasant working environment.

The second group that bears the brunt of popular frustrations are the workers in collective enterprises, which have mushroomed within the past five years. The popular image is that, due to more flexible management practices than in the state-owned factories, these enterprises are turning over huge profits and are distributing handsome bonuses to their employees. This is true of a highly publicized small minority of firms, but the reality of the situation, according to government statistics, is that the average annual income of the 34 million collective employees in 1986 was only 1,092 yuan, 322 yuan less than the earnings of the 93 million state-employed workers. Even the collective workers employed in foreign-run or joint-venture enterprises averaged only 1,629 yuan, just 200 yuan more than those in state enterprises. Moreover, collective employees normally work harder during work hours, do not enjoy as many fringe benefits and have less job security than those in the state-run sector.

The third group which is said to be making a lot of money are the peasants. This is a grossly distorted picture. The peasants who are doing well are those whom the urban people come into contact with—those who reside in the suburban counties. Through vegetable sales and the like, they can afford consumer goods today and live in less cramped accommodation than city dwellers. But these peasants are a small minority. The reality is that, like many other developing countries, China suffers from a noticeable urban bias. In 1986, while the average net income of a peasant was 424 yuan, an urbanite received 1,329 yuan, a ratio of 1:3. Slightly more than half of a peasant household's net income goes toward food, and there is little disposable cash income left for other necessities. Moreover, peasants do not receive most of the social benefits that are provided to the urban populace. In earlier decades, they did enjoy some rudimentary medical insurance at the collective's expense. Today, after de-collectivization, with the general deterioration of collective social institutions, especially in poor areas, even these have disappeared. Peasants do not receive any pension, and have to provide their own housing, which has always devoured the lion's share of their life-time savings.

It is therefore surprising that these three groups are singled out by interviewees as the recipients of unduly high incomes, while there are groups which are making ten, twenty, even a hundred times more than the national average income (more about these groups later). A possible explanation is that all of these three groups have had very low status in socialist China. For many years, a state-sector job had been the most sought after. A job with a collective enterprise was second best. No matter how Maoist ideology had attempted to raise the status of the peasants, it was ingrained in the popular consciousness that the peasants were still at the bottom of the heap. The 'private household' trades, for their part, had been abolished back in the 1950s and were allowed to revive only in the early 1980s as a measure to reduce urban unemployment. Initially, only the retired elderly and unemployed young people were willing to start a private endeavour. It was regarded as a stop-gap livelihood for those who could not participate in the state-sector mainstream. Only a few years back, in 1982, in one survey of senior high school graduates, out of 38 job categories the self-employed worker ranked last in desirability.[4] The animosity and envy felt by interviewees should be understood in these terms: the feeling that suddenly, within the space of a few years, all of these lowly people without any respectable skills are making more money—undeservedly.

The Intellectuals—How Much are they Worth?

Those most resentful of these lowly groups are the 'intellectuals'. In Chinese, the term encompasses a wide range of professions, from nuclear physicists through factory technicians to primary school teachers. As a group they have been articulate and vocal in recent years in agitating for higher pay. Primary and secondary school teachers are indeed quite poorly paid, so low that there is now a great staff shortage and teachers' training colleges have difficulty recruiting students. But the most vociferous demands for more pay come from the university teachers and research personnel, the 'high-level intellectuals'. Now that modernization, not revolution, is said to be the route to China's salvation, academics and professionals openly argue that their mental labour is worth considerably more than manual labour.

They claim repeatedly in print and in conversations that they are being discriminated against; that their salary is so low that they suffer from malnutrition; that because they work and read at home at night they are entitled to better housing; that middle- and high-level intellectuals tend to die prematurely compared to the national mortality rate; that those who suffer most are middle-aged intellectuals groaning under the financial burdens of elderly parents and children.

This chorus of complaints notwithstanding, academics are actually doing somewhat better financially, not worse, than the average worker. Among the eight occupational groups in the civil service pay scale, academics rank second highest, after state-organ officials. National statistics show, moreover, that the status and influence of the intellectuals have greatly improved in the past ten years. Of the ten million personnel with 'special technocratic skills' (excluding primary and secondary school teachers), about three million have received awards or recognition of various types, 30 per cent have joined the Communist Party, one million have taken up leadership positions in the Party, and 50,000 have gone abroad to study for extended periods, a figure that does not include the many academics and cultural and administrative personnel who have been able to travel abroad on shorter visits.

Whilst the government is under pressure to provide salaries commensurate with the improved status of intellectuals, it remains unwilling to dig deep into the state budget to raise their salaries substantially. Consequently, for several years now the government has allowed academics and professionals to supplement their incomes by taking up second jobs full-time or part-time. So far 14 per cent of the ten million have done so.[5] In the past year, the government has also begun encouraging university departments to institute a 'create income' programme, under which departments are free to run businesses or offer services to enterprises to supplement departmental budgets. The extra income is divided among the university administration, the department and the faculty and staff. Through this, Qinghua University in Beijing was able to distribute a 600 to 1,000 yuan bonus to each faculty and staff member at the end of 1987.[6] In primary and secondary schools, teachers selling snacks to students after class is a common sight. Weak objections from some quarters have been drowned out by the policy's popularity with the teaching profession. But the very fact that the academics and professionals have to take on extra work on the side to make ends meet has become a sore point among them.

The Workers—Losing the Iron Rice Bowl

Workers have their own fair share of grievances, as they see their previously superior status challenged and manual labour relegated to a position inferior to mental labour. All the while, their job security and handsome fringe benefits are progressively crumbling. For a number of years after the introduction of the reforms their wages were buoyed by bonuses handed out by factory managements eager to seem benevolent. But these wage increases are being eaten away now by a sharply rising inflation. Increasingly, the reforms have come to mean to them tighter control over work schedules, a raising of work quotas, monetary penalties for shoddy work, redundancy, even unemployment. The new system of contracting out enterprises to individuals, which is due to spread across the country, has tended to bring labour reductions in its wake. While a law permitting bankruptcies continues to be debated heatedly within the national leadership, the jobs of many workers in state enterprises and collective enterprises have already been put on the line.

The skilled workers can take advantage of the emerging free labour market to job-hop, and in some trades their incomes have increased substantially in the process. But to the ordinary unskilled and semi-skilled workers, threatened by job insecurity, a free labour market is a mixed blessing. Nationwide there are now 30 million surplus workers, about a quarter of the urban workforce.[7] By one estimate, economic streamlining in the next few years will render 10 to 20 million redundant. Once laid off they will have to compete for jobs with 30 million new arrivals to the labour market, a figure that does not include the uncountable number of rural migrants who have begun crowding into the urban areas. The future prospects are dim, in short, for a sizeable number of workers. Within the next few years China will likely be burdened by high unemployment.

In these circumstances, it is not surprising that when the intellectuals incessantly complain in print that their working conditions are arduous and that their salaries and housing conditions ought to be considerably better than the industrial workforce's, they arouse the workers' resentment.

The Peasants—Entering Troubled Times

Even though the lot of the peasants improved after 1978, their living standards are still far below those of the urban populace. To a large extent this is due to a pricing system that is biased against agricultural products *vis-à-vis* manufactured goods. The current 'contract' system for grain still binds many peasants to deliver grain at an artificially depressed price. Moreover, the soaring price of agricultural inputs has been cancelling out much of the peasants' remaining gains. In the isolated and backward areas where farmers have to live almost entirely off grain production, living conditions have barely improved or have actually dropped. In one impoverished county in Shanxi in 1985, peasants who concentrated on grain only made 100 yuan per capita a year, one-third of the average rural income for the county, and one-quarter of the national peasant average of 397 yuan.[8]

The 120 million peasants who eke out a subsistence living

in the poorest parts of China's hinterlands, in regions where industrial development is negligible, hold little chance of seeing their conditions improved under the government's current urban-biased and seaboard-biased development plans. Indeed, their income is projected to lag even further behind in the coming years.

The several hundreds of millions of peasants within striking distance of urban markets are doing far better. Freeing them to pursue their sideline endeavours, and the return of a free market in the early 1980s succeeded in raising their incomes substantially. These increases cannot be sustained year after year, however, without capital investments. Yet, the present government's policy is to concentrate on industrial modernization and to let the peasants pull themselves up by their own boot-straps. From 1980 to 1986, the share of capital investments in agriculture declined from 9.3 per cent to 3.3 per cent of the national budget. In a similar fashion, within the villages, private funds are being diverted away from agriculture and into more lucrative endeavours. The effects are already becoming apparent. The rural irrigation systems are deteriorating, land is being depleted, agricultural machinery is old and in disrepair, and there is a serious shortage of expert agricultural personnel.

Grain production has begun sliding after reaching a record high in 1984. By 1987 shortages of pork had reappeared, and ration tickets for meat and other essentials had to be reintroduced. To avert a crisis in food supplies, the government in 1988 moved to increase procurement prices for pork and other foodstuffs. But investment in agriculture under the Seventh Five-Year Plan remains a low 5 per cent of the state's budget.

Whilst the intellectuals and workers have gained some ground under the reforms in freeing themselves from the yoke of bureaucratic control, the peasants have been less fortunate. A popular image is that with the dissolution of the collective system, the state has been lifted off the peasants' backs. The reality is that whereas many of the positive features of the collective system have been destroyed, the peasants are still very much under the thumbs of local cadres. The cadres no longer organize the peasants' daily work routine, but as one western scholar puts it, 'cadres have not so much lost power as refocused it. The personalized authority of cadres and clientelistic politics characteristic of the pre-reform period have not been eliminated: they have merely taken on a different form'.[9] They continue to hold substantial control over the peasants' lives, especially in their discretionary power over the distribution of agricultural inputs and other materials. Rather than a relatively free system of small-scale entrepreneurship emerging in the countryside, the economic reforms have opened the door to new forms of patronage relationships that benefit the local officialdom.

The New Monied Elite—the True Winners

While none of the broad social groups sees itself today as having made dramatic gains under the economic reforms, a new stratum that could be termed a 'monied élite' has arisen under the government's slogan that 'some should get rich first'. They are the '10,000-yuan households', the owners of 'private enterprises' (*siren qiye*), the lessee-managers of state and collective enterprises, and lastly, officials and their offspring who have set themselves up as private middlemen in commodity sales. They are, for China, the counterparts of the multi-millionaires of capitalist economies.

The '10,000-yuan households' are, for the most part, peasants or village officials who started off accumulating capital as 'specialized households'—households which had acquired permission to free themselves from the burden of unprofitable grain-production contracts so as to be able to concentrate on lucrative industrial, agricultural or service industries.

'Private enterprises' are officially defined as those employing eight or more workers. Their owners sometimes began humbly as 'private households', but they also include the families of officials who have taken advantage of their influence to acquire the required licences and capital. Today there are 225,000 private enterprises, employing some 3.6 million workers in all.[10] During the past few years their size and scope have expanded rapidly, some having acquired capital assets of well over a million yuan. For some years these enterprises have been basking in the glow of *'laissez faire* socialism', taking advantage of lax enterprise laws to evade taxes. Only in June 1988 did the State Council first publish tax laws with some teeth in them, simultaneously decreeing that the incomes of owners and managers be limited to a maximum of ten times the average income of their employees (whether these laws are enforceable or not is another matter). To offset these new restrictions, the inheritability of private holdings has been guaranteed in law.

The endeavours of these two new groups of monied élites are essentially 'capitalistic' in character. The third and fourth groups, on the other hand, are the products of the hybrid planned/free market economy, in line with a new 'socialist' concept that makes much of a distinction between ownership rights and use rights. Thus the third group within the new monied élite are the so-called 'lessees' of public enterprises who, at some personal financial risk, guarantee to generate increased profits for the firms they take over. More often than not, the 'lessee-managers' had been Communist Party secretaries or directors of the very same enterprises under state management. So lucrative has this 'leasing-management' practice become that a heated debate on whether it constitutes 'capitalism' has cropped up in the public press. The lessees have been referred to sarcastically as 'capitalists without capital', meaning that they operate as capitalists without even having to furnish their own initial capital. Oddly, this same question has not been asked of the first two means of amassing wealth, which are more clearly 'capitalistic' in nature.

The fourth type of endeavour that generates high personal profits tends to be monopolized by the political élite and their offspring. Much of their economic activities involves the running of 'trading companies' in China, in the SEZs, or in Hong Kong. A good deal of China's import-export trade, among other things, passes through these private 'companies', and very handsome rake-offs occur. A surprisingly large number of the children of the national leadership run such trading companies. In many respects they are 'socialist compradors', the equivalents of the pre-Liberation compradors who were labelled as hated 'enemies of the people' when the communist government first took power.

A majority of the new monied élite seems to be drawn from the families of the powers-that-be at all bureaucratic levels. Their power is now enhanced by wealth. Popular resentment is running high against these officials and their kin. Sarcastic sayings abound like 'to be rich you have to have been an official' and 'the road to riches is to quit being a county head and become

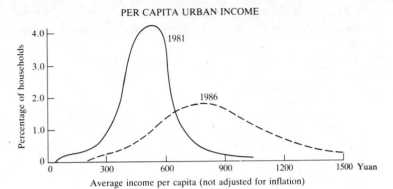

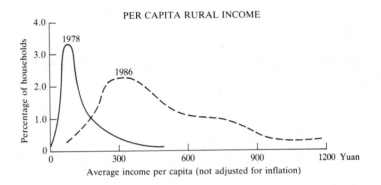

a factory manager'. Towards the self-made *nouveaux riches*, however, resentment is more subdued and is often mixed with respect. There is as yet no open objection to the emergence of genuine 'capitalism' and 'capitalists' *per se*; what irks ordinary Chinese is the lack of equal opportunity for all to partake in the scramble.

The Widening Income Gap

That, in only a matter of a few years, the income gap in China has widened considerably is well illustrated in this graph from China's 1987 Statistical Yearbook.[11]

But such statistics have not put the reformers on the defensive. The 'get rich first' slogan and the more recent ideological catchphrase 'China is still in the primary stage of socialism' have been nailed in place to counter any criticism. In fact, Su Shaozhi, the former director of the Marxism–Leninism–Mao–Zedong-Thought Institute of the Chinese Academy of Social Sciences, an authoritative ideologue of the reform faction, argues:

> Under the violent stimulation of the mechanism of market competition, the emergence of *great* disparity in income is *inevitable*. The disparity is natural. As long as the majority of society's members are benefiting from the reforms (although the speed at which prosperity is attained varies), we should not be afraid of this kind of disparity [italics added].[12]

Truly excessive differences between rich and poor, Su argues, can be avoided through taxation and welfare programmes.

Whether taxation *could* effectively redistribute wealth in China remains to be seen. Tax laws relating to personal income and private enterprises were instituted respectively in 1987 and 1988. But with the current widespread practice of tax evasion in China, even if a regularized tax mechanism could take root it will require considerable time for it to develop.

As for using welfare as a levelling mechanism, the irony is that China's economic reforms are rapidly dismantling the socialist welfare system. In the past few years, state and local funding for hospitals and medical services has dwindled, and medical institutions are being asked to fend for themselves by raising charges. The 90 per cent of China's populace outside the state-employed sector who have never enjoyed free medical services are now threatened with astronomical bills. The proposed scenario is that a new system of medical insurance paid for by the work unit and/or the individual will be put in place to alleviate the burdens faced by families. Notwithstanding this, a sizeable part of the urban population will remain uninsured.

In the sphere of education, too, the reform policies are shifting the financial burdens on to the collectives and private shoulders. The first casualties are the poor rural areas, which are witnessing primary-school closures and a declining student body. In higher education, as seen already, funding to fully cover staff salaries has not been forthcoming. Instead, to raise more money, special places are now set aside in universities for 'independent students', those who can pay their own annual tuition of 1,800–

2,000 yuan, a sum in excess of an average worker's yearly income. Obviously, this new recruitment policy opens the door of higher education wider to the children of the monied élite, who otherwise would have had difficulty entering university by way of the cut-throat national university entrance examinations.

Reforms in the provision of housing similarly favour the monied élite and impinge adversely on the interests of ordinary urban families. Ostensibly inaugurated to raise funds to ease the current housing shortage and to stamp out corrupt practices in the distribution of housing, a newly proposed system would raise rents by about 500 per cent. The overall result will be to squeeze the lower-salaried families into smaller living units, opening up the larger flats for wealthy families at high rentals. The new policies also encourage wealthy families to purchase new flats at several tens of thousands of yuan apiece. Understandably, as one Chinese report observes, the impending policies are 'grating on people's most sensitive nerves'.[13]

Fuelled by inflation, all of these new social policies are eroding the material well-being of low- and even middle-income families. The most recent national figures are for 1986, and in that year 161 million people qualified for state-funded social relief, a 7.3 per cent increase over the previous year. Of these, 15 million were urban poor, a surprising jump of 65 per cent from the previous year. Though eligible for relief, only a small percentage received any: 2 per cent of the urban poor and 39 per cent of the rural poor.[14]

Consequently, a large group of very under-privileged urban poor is in the making. Their numbers are rapidly being supplemented from the countryside, where Chinese estimates show a labour surplus of some 30–40 per cent. The tens of millions of peasants who have swarmed into the cities and market towns in recent years are taking up the most menial and heavy jobs, sometimes legally, sometimes illegally. As one example, in Guangdong province as early as 1982 shows, a third of a million peasants were working without legal authorization in urban state enterprises.[15] In Beijing, migrants make up 12 per cent of the population; and a third of these migrants sleep at construction sites.

Of greater concern is the situation in China's county towns, where sweatshops operate with no need to observe labour laws.

Child labour, drawing on the children of impoverished peasants, constitutes about 10 per cent of the industrial workforce in some counties, according to official reports.

Proposals to Avert a Crisis

It can be argued that Su Shaozhi's solution of taxation and welfare to narrow the widening gap in incomes is not realistic. At least for the time being, reform policies are working diametrically against such a scenario; and even were an effort to be made, China's poverty and desperate population pressures defy a comprehensive welfare system. But Su's line of reasoning has become the reform faction's argument against any potential objections to economic polarization.

The media is dominated by an ethos that lashes out at any notion of egalitarianism, discrediting it as 'ultra-leftist', as manifesting an 'eating-from-one-big-pot mentality', and incompatible with the reforms. Some commentators do point out that great disparities in income distribution are 'unreasonable', implying that it is not historically determined and therefore something can be done to avoid it; but such a view is accompanied by statements carefully distinguishing between 'equalitarianism', which is bad, and a 'reasonable disparity of wealth' which is good. Today, when advancing any views, one has to be careful not to be tagged as an advocate of 'equalitarianism'.

One school of thought perceives China to be undergoing a process of human relocation, social restructuring and stratification on a scale as massive as the Industrial Revolution in the West. Seeing the situation as more critical than Su does, such commentators fear social instability. To avert this, they advocate granting interest groups legal status and institutional means to channel their frustrations and to fight out their conflicts in the open, much as Hungary had done in the 1960s. Others call for caution, a slowing down of the reform policies, a moratorium on efforts that promote a widening of the income gap. But such arguments are aimed at economic efficiency and crisis-aversion rather than being appeals to social justice. Some researchers and reporters write on behalf of the peasants who have fallen by the wayside, but implicit in their writings is the realization that these are desperate cries in the wilderness.

Social Restructuring and Articulation of Political Interests

A new social and economic structure inevitably gives rise to a realignment of political forces. Professional associations and kindred organizations, chambers of commerce, philanthropic foundations and learned societies have mushroomed in the order of thousands since the beginning of the reforms. They are not the 'mass organizations' of yesteryear. These actively lobby for their own interests quite independent of Communist Party control. Their activities range from fund-raising concerts, suicide-prevention hot-lines, signature campaigns, to Gallup-poll type social surveys—a nascent civil society is emerging in China. There is *de facto*, if not yet official, recognition of interest group politics.

This was evident at the 7th National People's Congress (NPC) and the 7th Chinese People's Political Consultative Conference (CPPCC), both of which convened in the spring of 1988. Though still largely rubber-stamp political institutions, they nonetheless were the most open in the history of the People's Republic of China. The press was granted unprecedented liberty to cover the conferences. 'Abstention' votes and 'no' votes, critical speeches by delegates, attitudinal interviews with passers-by in the street were all reported in straightforward fashion. To be sure, the delegates had all been 'elected' via Communist Party selection, or with its approval, but in the late 1980s they find it incumbent upon themselves to speak up for the interests of the groups they were told to represent.

Not all social groups, however, are given proportional representation in this political arena. The group which is disproportionately represented are the intellectuals, in particular the high-level intellectuals—university professors, writers, researchers, cultural celebrities, technocrats and professionals. Their representatives tend to hold nationally recognized names in their own fields of expertise. The groups that have been apportioned relatively few delegates—an indicator of the priorities of the top Party leadership—are the peasantry and industrial workforce. Of the 2,081 delegates to the 7th CPPCC, at least 925 can definitely be identified as representing intellectuals, while a mere 85 sit as representatives for the 'agricultural and forestry sector', and 64 for the 'trade unions'. Of the remaining delegates for miscellaneous groups such as 'returned overseas Chinese', most seem also to be prominent intellectuals.[16]

At the 7th NPC, the peasants and workers were only slightly better represented. Out of 2,970 delegates, the sectoral representation for workers and peasants comprised 23 per cent of the assemblage, intellectuals 23 per cent, officials 25 per cent and the army 9 per cent. At the national NPC, each rural delegate represents eight times as many 'electors' as delegates from the urban areas; at the provincial level, five times more. Worse yet, in this sectoral representation format, the rural delegate is likely to be a recent success story, a '10,000-yuan household', a member of the new monied élite whose interests are apt to be at odds with his less fortunate brethren. One rural delegate complained that there are several tens of millions of people in Gansu province who do not have enough grain to eat, yet little had been discussed regarding China's agricultural problems.

Two kinds of delegates stole the limelight at the congresses: the intellectuals, large in number and articulate, whose views on education and complaints about their own low wages were widely covered by the press; and the monied élite, the new successful entrepreneurs held up as models to be admired and emulated nationwide.

The intellectuals above all are allowed to operate through an organizational structure that has some semblance to political parties. These are the Democratic Parties (DPs), one of which represents the high-level intellectuals, another specifically the technocrats and scientists, another the doctors, another school teachers, and yet others the overseas Chinese, Taiwanese and people with former Kuomintang connections. There are eight DPs in all, and the eighth, the Democratic National Construction Association, is reserved for private industrialists and businessmen. Also representing them is the All-China Federation of Industry and Commerce, an organization of pre-1949 businessmen (founded in 1953) which today has a membership of over half a million and which has been enrolled as a constituent member of the increasingly influential Chinese People's Political Consultative Conference.

The DPs explicitly see their role as serving their membership's interests. As Fei Xiaotong, China's best-known social scientist and chairman of the Democratic Alliance, the biggest of the DPs, proclaims:

> Under the leadership of the Communist Party, we Democratic Parties represent the basic levels of society as interest groups. The Democratic Alliance represents the interests of intellectuals and especially intellectuals involved in teaching. We want to express their opinions and also to do everything we can to protect their interests.[17]

The membership of the eight DPs has nearly tripled this past decade, climbing to 160,000 by 1986. Since 6,900 People's Congress and CPPCC deputies at the national and provincial levels are DP members, at least one out of every 23 DP members has become a delegate to an influential official forum.

For several decades the DPs had been widely dismissed as ineffectual historical vestiges and handmaidens of the Communist Party, but once allowed to be revitalized in the 1980s these hybrid professional associations cum political parties have become high-prestige alternatives to Communist Party membership for ambitious intellectuals. One has to attain a certain professional and social standing before one can receive an invitation to join one. In Kunming, the newly-built Democratic Parties–People's Political Consultative Conference headquarters is the most luxurious public building in the city, complete with western executive-style suites. In interviews, a sense of self-importance is obvious among leaders of the city's Democratic Parties.

Already, some members of the DPs are asking for a guaranteed number of seats in the National People's Congress and are even seeking an amalgamated *en bloc* representation for all of the eight parties. (This request appears to have been inspired by recent political developments in Taiwan, where after years of struggle independent 'non-KMT' (*dangwai*) politicians were finally allowed to form an opposition party two years ago.) The boldest power-sharing aspirations emanate from the new monied élite: within the Democratic National Construction Association there has even been open discussion of the feasibility of forming a genuine opposition political party. But however aggressive their demands, the intellectual establishment and the new monied élite limit themselves to operating firmly within the status quo.

Some of the university students, however, are too impatient to work within the system. Annually these past few years, students have taken to the streets, each time plunging the national political leadership into a flutter of anxiety. The students' demonstrations have proved ineffectual in drawing popular support, however, because their demands either have been too idealistic and vague, in support of such things as 'Freedom', or too narrowly drawn, such as protests demanding better on-campus security against crime. Thus far, the student demonstrations have served largely as safety-valves, not ultimately threatening to the government.

This safety-valve formula does not apply to the peasants and workers. Theoretically represented by the Communist Party, worker-peasant interests are not provided with alternative outlets. Thus far, workers have not taken to strikes and have not agitated for independent trade unions à la Solidarity, but the authorities are well aware of the 'threshold of endurance', a worrying term recently much used in the press. The worst scenario, so far as the leadership is concerned, would be for students and workers to join hands in taking to the streets together. When the student demonstrations at the end of 1986 began to attract throngs of workers as on-lookers, the demonstrations were quickly and forcibly brought to a halt.

Unable to articulate their grievances in words, the peasantry have been venting their frustrations in disorganized ways. For instance, when the officials responsible for chemical-fertilizer production created a deliberate fertilizer shortage in 1987 in order to jack up prices, several million peasants took the law into their own hands in 100,000 separate incidents, looting fertilizer plants and waylaying lorries.[18] This wave of violence is reflective of a society torn by tensions, and a government that is losing control over its own functionaries and people.

The honeymoon years between the Deng Xiaoping administration and the Chinese people are over. China's social and moral fabric is under challenge from the enormous economic changes that are being put in place by a government that has proved itself far more concerned with economic development than equity. Those who see themselves as the losers are worried and growing impatient. Ordinary people increasingly perceive the officialdom as morally bankrupt, and believe that the large portion of the new monied élite that has ties to bureaucracy is attaining its wealth through illegitimate means. A troubled decade for China lies ahead.

1. To absorb the shock, each urban resident (excluding teenagers and children) henceforth will receive a subsidy of some 10 yuan a month to partially cover the new increases in food costs. *Beijing Review*, 23 May, 1988, p. 6. (For the convenience of readers, references are made in my notes, wherever possible, to English-language sources.)
2. *Beijing Review*, 13 June, 1988, p. 5.
3. *China News Analysis*, No. 1339 (15 July, 1987), p. 1.
4. Lan Chengdong and Zhang Zhongru, 'Aspirations and Inclinations of this Year's Senior High School Graduates', *Chinese Sociology and Anthropology*, Vol. XVI, No. 1–2 (Fall–Winter 1983–84), p. 38.
5. *China Daily*, 28 May, 1988, p. 3.
6. *Renmin Ribao*, 13 April, 1988, p. 1.
7. *Beijing Review*, 29 June, 1988, p. 7.
8. *China News Analysis*, No. 1323 (1 December, 1986), p. 3.
9. Jean Oi, 'Commercializing China's Rural Cadres', *Problems of Communism*, September–October, 1986, p. 2.
10. *Beijing Review*, 18 July, 1988, p. 6. This figure is actually on the low side since an unknown number of private enterprises are registered as 'collective enterprises'.
11. *Zhongguo Tongji Nianjian 1987* (China Statistical Yearbook 1987), Beijing, China Statistical Publishing Co., 1987, pp. 714–5.
12. Su Shaozhi and Wang Yizhou, 'The Two Major Historical Missions of the Reforms', *Renmin Ribao*, 5 March, 1988, p. 5.
13. *Renmin Ribao*, 9 October, 1988, p. 2.
14. *Handbook of China Population References* (in Chinese), Beijing, Population Information Center, 1987, pp. 320–3.
15. Wojtek Zanfanolli, 'A Brief Outline of China's Second Economy', *Asian Survey*, Vol. XXV, No. 7 (July 1985), p. 727. As of 1986 another 200,000 Guangdong peasants from poverty-stricken districts had moved into the delta areas to rent land, entering into share-cropping relationships with local households who can make a better living outside agriculture. These migrants live in make-shift tents or pigsties without any security of tenancy. Hein Mallee, 'Rural–Urban Migration Control in the People's Republic of China: Effects of the Recent Reforms', *China Information* (Leiden), Vol. I, No. 4 (Spring 1988), pp. 16–17.
16. See *Renmin Zhengxie Bao* (The People's Political Consultative Committee Newspaper), 8 March, 1988, p. 1, which lists the number of delegates from each group. I have classed all the representatives from the Democratic Parties as 'intellectuals'.
17. *Inside China Mainland*, June 1988, p. 24.
18. *China Daily*, 22 April, 1988, p. 4, and *Shehui* (Society), No. 2 (March 1987), pp. 14–15.

6. The Chinese People's Liberation Army: 1949–89

HARLAN W. JENCKS

THE Chinese revolution was made with the essential help of the armed forces of the Communist Party. In the forty years since the revolution, the armed forces have fought various wars abroad, and played a key part in maintaining law and order at home. It was the first communist army to intervene in politics and it has regularly been beset by disagreements over the extent of professionalism. After the death of Mao, the armed forces began their second revolution, including a withdrawal from politics, greater professionalism and the adoption of new military doctrines. But as long as civilian politics remain uncertain, it also remains possible that the army will enter politics and politics will enter the army. The dilemmas of the Chinese armed forces have a lengthy history.

Military Operations 1949–54

By late 1949, the People's Liberation Army (PLA) was in sole control of vast areas of southern and western china, where the Communist Party infrastructure was weak or nonexistent. The army carried the administrative burden alone. This situation continued through the spring of 1950, as the PLA completed the military conquest of Hainan Island and prepared to enter Tibet. Civilian control was officially established throughout China by the constitution of 1954, but many high-ranking military officers remained in charge of provinces and regions because they held simultaneous party and/or government posts. This situation persisted until the end of the 1970s. Demobilization of the PLA began in late 1949, but was halted by China's entry into the Korean War in late 1950.[1]

As the PLA's initial advance into Korea was halted by UN forces, its military shortcomings began to show. American artillery and air power pounded PLA supply lines. Peng Dehuai, the Chinese commander, found his logistical system almost entirely dependent upon human porters who hauled supplies and ammunition over the bleak mountains in darkness. PLA troop morale suffered as they operated for the first time on foreign soil. By the end of the Korean fighting, Russian advisers, equipment and methods had superseded the light infantry traditions of many PLA units. The political commissar and party committee systems within military units had proven dysfunctional in conventional war on foreign soil, and deteriorated badly.[2]

Because of his logistical situation, Peng Dehuai's only abundant resource was manpower, which he used lavishly. His 'human wave' attacks were regarded in the west as 'typically Chinese', though they were actually unusual in PLA history. The PLA had traditionally heeded Sun Tzu's admonition to 'strike where the enemy is weakest', but in the narrow confines of the Korean peninsula, that was often impossible. Moreover, 'human wave' tactics had a political advantage: many PLA units which entered Korea in 1950 and 1951 were essentially Nationalist units which had defected late in the civil war. Though reorganized and seeded with political officers, their political reliability was uncertain. Demobilization of these units would have been tricky. Thus, to some extent, UN firepower in Korea rid the new regime of a potentially dangerous political problem.

The Korean War showed the world that the PLA soldier was tough, disciplined and generally well-motivated. The awesome firepower of the UN forces, however, made a deep impression on PLA commanders. Peng became a leading advocate of rapid 'modernization' and 'regularization' to meet the challenge.

In September 1949, PLA units had landed on Quemoy Island, just off the coast of Fujian, but were repelled. The Korean War placed Taiwan operations on hold, but in early 1954, the party Military Affairs Commission (MAC) agreed upon the principle of 'liberating China's offshore islands from small to large, one island at a time, from north to south, from weak to strong'.[3] The plan did not call for a renewed attack on Quemoy or Matsu, but the PLA launched an artillery attack on Quemoy on 3 September 1954. The United States was on the verge of concluding a mutual defence treaty with the Republic of China (ROC) on Taiwan, and the attack was a message to Washington.

On 1 November the PLA landed on Yijiangshan Island, north-ernmost of the ROC-held islands, and finally secured it on 18 January 1955. Meanwhile, the United States and the ROC signed a treaty extending American protection to Taiwan and the Penghu Islands. The treaty did not extend protection to any of the other offshore islands, and Washington publicly pressured the ROC to evacuate the Tachens. PLA leaders on the spot urged an immediate attack to destroy Nationalist forces during the evacuation. After some debate in Beijing, however, the MAC ordered them to desist and allow evacuation. On 14 February, the PLA occupied the Tachens unopposed. This 'Taiwan Straits crisis' of 1954–55, as it came to be known, did not involve any direct PRC–American military clash, partly because Chinese troops were under strict orders to avoid any provocative action toward American forces.

Modernizing on the Russian Model

Even as the fighting in Korea escalated, the PLA demobilized some of its less capable military formations, including virtually all the militia units activated late in the civil war. Some became People's Armed Forces Police units, controlled by the Ministry of Public Security after 1954. The mid-1950s saw all China striving to be 'modern and Soviet'. The PLA established insti-tutional links with the Soviet Defence Ministry and Peng Dehuai, Minister of Defence under the new constitution, estab-lished a working relationship with Marshal Zhukov, his Russian counterpart. Abandoning the PLA's volunteer tradition, con-scription began in September 1954. The 'Sovietized' complexion of the PLA was dramatized in February 1955, when the PLA adopted a Soviet system of military rank and Russian-style uniforms.

The PLA set up a comprehensive Soviet-style system of pro-fessional officer education. This was the first of many reforms that would be necessary to transform what was still essentially a light infantry force into a professional modern army. The navy, air force, and armoured forces, which had been essentially nonexistent during the civil war, were most easily cast in the Soviet mould. Infantry forces, on the other hand, retained tra-ditional PLA methods, structures, and mentalities. For example, infantry officers were theoretically required to attend higher military schools to be promoted, but the requirement was widely ignored. In 1954 PLA ground units began reorganizing along Soviet lines. About half had converted to standard organizations before the process was interrupted by the 'Great Leap Forward' and the loss of Soviet aid. This left the PLA partly composed of modified units with substandard equipment, a situation that still persists.

The Soviets were generous allies, providing the PLA with their latest military technology. MiG-17 fighters, *Osa*-class patrol boats and T-55 tanks, for example, almost simultaneously entered Chinese and Soviet service. With Soviet assistance, the first jet fighters were produced in 1956. By 1957, China was essentially self-sufficient in weapons up to about 90 mm.

Peng Dehuai began a systematic assault on the militia system. He ordered a 10–30 per cent cutback in militia strength and recalled most of its weapons. Meanwhile, he began organizing Soviet-style 'army reserve divisions' with which he intended ultimately to replace the militia. Peng's military policies were apparently aimed at decreasing defence expenditures by reliance on a well-trained reserve. The savings would be invested in industrial development and military modernization. This implicitly required, for the foreseeable future, Chinese reliance on the Soviet Union for technical aid and a 'nuclear umbrella'.[4]

The Soviet Model Reconsidered

In his September 1956 report to the 8th Party Congress, Peng described technical training of officers, technicians and troops as 'the central routine work in our army'.[5] Radical Maoists subsequently claimed that Peng intended to create a carbon copy of the Soviet Army, and to compromise party leadership by replacing it with Soviet-style 'one-man command'. The Soviet model, however, provides ultimate party control by indoctrinating and co-opting the officer corps. This was apparently what Peng, a lifelong revolutionary, had in mind.

Although the PLA officer corps voiced no public criticism during the 'Hundred Flowers' movement, Mao Zedong evidently feared military dissent. Many junior military officers were purged in 1957. Mao also disapproved of the way the officer corps had strayed from the PLA's egalitarian traditions. Chinese officers had begun to exhibit some of the bad habits of KMT and warlord officers. In 1958, families of officers were ordered back to their home villages, thereby ridding PLA garrisons of a leading source of officer-enlisted friction. In September 1958, a movement was launched for officers to 'go down to the companies and soldier' (*xialian dangbing*). Every officer had to spend a month per year serving as a common soldier. The movement was launched just as China began the 'Great Leap Forward'. Also in 1958–59, radicals attacked military academies as bastions of foreign influence and caste consciousness. Peng Dehuai's opposition to the 'Great Leap Forward' is well known. He was particularly disturbed by its disruptive effect on the national defence industry, and by the decline in military morale because of soldiers' concerns about their families.

September 1958 saw the first visible crack in the Sino-Soviet military alliance. The United States supported the Nationalists during the second Taiwan Straits crisis, in marked contrast to the cautious, grudging Soviet backing for Beijing. If there had been any doubts before, the crisis certainly convinced Mao and the Central Committee that they needed an independent nuclear capability.[6] Soviet inaction also weakened Peng Dehuai's political position, since he had become identified with the Soviet alliance. He was further weakened because his air force, after seven years of Soviet tutelage, took a beating at the hands of Nationalist pilots.

Another damaging affect of the 'Great Leap Forward' on the PLA was the 'everyone a soldier' movement. Regional forces devoted their full time to militia training, but the militia was under local party control. Here, Mao Zedong clearly overruled Peng on a military issue. Peng's reserve scheme was disregarded while formations of workers and peasants drilled with bayonets and spears. Worse, the PLA was blamed late in 1959 when the militia expansion flopped. There were 'paper' militia units, corruption, and even cases of units taking their weapons and becoming bandits.

Peng was purged at the Lushan plenum of August 1959. His opposition to Mao's economic policies and to the mass militia had made enemies of Mao and his followers, as had his close identification with the Soviets. In fact, the Russians may have administered the *coup de grâce* to Peng by repudiating the 1958 nuclear power-sharing arrangement in June.[7] That action also confirmed the fears of senior soldiers like Marshals Ye Jianying, Nie Rongzhen, and Liu Bocheng and General Su Yu, who had opposed Peng's heavy reliance on the Soviet Union. They had advocated maintenance of larger Chinese forces against surprise attack. Marshal Lin Biao took over as Minister of National Defence (MND), and immediately did two things Peng had advocated: he reduced the militia and moderated the *xialian* campaign.

It is unclear how Lin Biao was picked as the new MND. He was acceptable to the PLA, since his credentials as a troop commander were impeccable. He had been ill during the mid-1950s, so he was unsullied by the political disagreements of that time. Given Lin's relatively professional training and career, and his past disagreements with Mao over military affairs, he was probably acceptable to Liu Shaoqi and Deng Xiaoping. He was 'red' enough to suit Mao and 'expert' enough to suit Liu. Moreover, Mao was in a weakened position at Lushan and hardly in a position to dictate who the new defence minister would be.

Between 1959 and 1963, Lin rebuilt the PLA party control system and 'placed politics in command'. In 1963, 'Political Work Regulations for the Chinese People's Liberation Army' codified the methods Lin had worked out embodying 'Maoist' mass-line principles. The Regulations addressed, in detail, basic issues of doctrine, organization, political work, and leadership.[8] The GPD published *Quotations from Chairman Mao*, the soon-to-be famous 'little red book', in 1964. Lin lost no opportunity to hail Mao's thought as a 'spiritual atomic bomb'.

In 1960–65, The Chinese Communist Party (CCP) went in two ideological directions. The 'expert' party, headed by Liu Shaoqi and Deng Xiaoping, operated within the civilian party apparatus. The 'red' party, dominated by Mao and Lin Biao, operated through the GPD and the party organization in the army. Mao decided to use the PLA as a model for the rest of China, and in early 1964 kicked off a movement to 'learn from the PLA in political and ideological work'. Military political officers organized political departments, along PLA lines, in government and

economic enterprises. This cut much of the political ground
from under Liu Shaoqi.

The invasion of the civilian sector by PLA commissars led to
factionalism within the army as well, because local party organs
and regional army units had worked closely over a decade.
Personal relationships had developed between local party and
military leaders, who both felt threatened by aggressive commissars. This situation set the stage for bloody confrontations
during the 'Cultural Revolution', when commissars and Red
Guards on one side battled commanders and local party organizations on the other.

The Case of Luo Ruiqing

Despite its political preparation, the PLA and the militia proved
far less radical during the 'Cultural Revolution' than might
have been expected. Behind the 'Maoist' rhetoric and political
retrenchment of the early 1960s, the PLA devoted most of its
time to normal military tasks. Lin Biao maintained a balance of
military and political work in his refurbishment of the army.
Training and readiness were the responsibility of the General
Staff Department (GSD) and its chief, Luo Ruiqing. Luo's position left him vulnerable to political attack when he and Lin
began to clash over strategic policies and domestic politics. Luo
was stripped of his power in November 1965 supposedly for
pursuing the 'bourgeois military line'. Actually, he was a career
political commissar who was less a military professional than
Lin Biao had been up to 1959. The real cause of Luo's downfall
was a bitter controversy over military security policy that
evolved as the Sino-Soviet rift widened and American involvement in Indo-China assumed threatening proportions. If the
Chinese decided to give North Vietnam full support, they would
have to repair the Sino-Soviet alliance to deter American
reprisals. Luo advocated doing this, and whether he realized it
or not, that placed him among Mao's domestic political enemies.
Liu Shaoqi was also calling for support of Hanoi and implicitly
for improved relations with Moscow.

In this context, Lin Biao delivered his famous speech of September 1965, 'Long Live the Victory of People's War!' By empha-
sizing self-sufficiency as *necessary* to a successful 'people's war',

Lin justified a low level of Chinese involvement in Vietnam while maintaining an ideologically defensible position *vis-à-vis* the Soviet Union.[9] Lin was speaking for Mao, who believed that embroilment in Vietnam was dangerous and unnecessary. Moreover, Mao had ideological and domestic political reasons for continuing the Sino-Soviet dispute. Even to suspend it would concede ideological points to Liu Shaoqi and the revisionists.

'People's War' rhetoric avoided direct involvement in Vietnam, and bought time for the further modernization of China's defences. Mao and Lin Biao worked out a balanced policy of people's war and force modernization, with propaganda emphasis on the former and resource priority to the latter. The policy stayed in effect until Mao's death in 1976, though the emphasis shifted steadily toward modernization. Lin Biao seems to have been the main architect of the balanced policy.

Despite Luo Ruiqing's dismissal, Chinese involvement in Indo-China grew, in a futile effort to counterbalance Soviet influence. Chinese aircraft continued to be the backbone of the North Vietnamese air force until late 1966, when Soviet aid surpassed China's.

The Cultural Revolution

In 1965, the top leadership of the PLA included both professionally inclined officers and others who were highly politicized. Junior and middle-level officers (recruited after about 1945) had spent most of their careers in rather professional, conventional military settings, both in combat and in garrison. The 'Cultural Revolution' was a severe test of these officers, in which they reacted in a remarkably military, as opposed to a politicized, manner. Like officers in many third-world states, they reacted to illegal or extra-legal challenges to the authority of the state by avoiding political involvement as much as possible. When finally forced to act, they tended to defend the status quo. At the end of the Cultural Revolution the PLA held the preponderance of political power in the country, and was slow to disengage itself because rapid military disengagement could easily have provoked another wave of radical violence.

The peak of the crisis came in the summer of 1967, when the PLA was confronted by virtually all of the conditions usually cited to justify a military *coup d'état*. Political factionalism had led to widespread civil disorder, the disruption of public services, economic stagnation, and the discrediting of civilian political institutions. Power was falling into the hands of unstable radicals who were hostile to the established social and political order. Military defences and defence industries were disrupted, as were strategic communications. Moreover, the radicals were trying to undermine the discipline of the armed forces. All of this seemed to invite foreign attack, particularly by the United States, which was pressing its war in Vietnam. In August 1967 a *coup d'état* could have been justified by virtually all the familiar motives associated with 'guardian' *coups*.[10] Instead of staging a *coup*, however, the PLA high command compromised with Mao Zedong, labelling a conservative solution with a radical name. Revolutionary Committees (RCs) were formed, generally run by the same military-political leaders from whom power had supposedly been 'seized'. Military Control Commissions forced radical Red Guards into 'great alliances' which had only token representation on the RCs.[11]

The army reasserted order in this comprehensive manner because of the determination of most military commanders, especially in the main forces, to minimize political involvement. Main force commissars and commanders alike believed that the party and army needed each other. At least the appearance of party control had to be maintained. The enemies of order were the Red Guards and their radical sponsors in the Central Cultural Revolution Group. A *coup d'état* would have been directed at the PLA's allies, the government and party, rather than its enemies.

Outright defiance of Central Committee (CC) orders was extremely rare among main force units. PLA commitment to party leadership repeatedly surfaced in the tendency of military leaders to defend party leaders and organs from Red Guard attack. Leaders of military regional (MR) commands, because they occupied borderline positions between civil and military, were far more prone to defy orders if local interests seemed threatened. Regional commissars were especially open to the temptation of attacking their commanders as a means of gaining local power and central favour. This was because regional commissars retained more clout than main force commissars, and also because the former were often 'civilians in uniform', who had not served in the military at all during the 1950s.

A few very strong regional leaders (notably Chen Xilian in Shenyang and Huang Yongsheng in Guangzhou) got into open conflicts, exposing themselves to attack from both 'right' and 'left'. They paid the price in civil disorder and near personal disaster.[12] Another factor, which may have operated in Shenyang and Guangzhou, was PLA generational conflict. In a number of cases, junior officers in regional units attempted to unseat their own superiors in an effort to create 'room at the top'.[13]

Of the entire high command, those most prone to 'warlordism' were MR commanders who, by concurrently holding key political posts, had dominated their regions for many years. They had made enough local enemies that they were threatened by any disturbance in the status quo. Two notable examples were Ulanfu in Inner Mongolia and Wang Enmao in Xinjiang, both of whom were simultaneously MR commander, MR commissar and provincial party first secretary. Ulanfu was removed in May 1967, but his followers were not finally suppressed (by main force units) until September. Wang suppressed Red Guards as well as the few main force units in his domain. In 1968, he finally relinquished his post as MR commander (only), while becoming a vice-chairman of the provincial RC.[14] Even these two never seem to have contemplated secession from the PRC or the establishment of competing national governments—despite being in geographical positions to appeal for Soviet assistance. Wang and Ulanfu were guilty of disobedience and resistance, but not of rebellion. This commitment to national and military unity was a crucial factor in the events of 1967. The high command realized that without central political authority, the PLA could fragment into a dozen or more regionally based factions; that could have meant civil war.

Even if the PLA could have been held together, a *coup d'état* would have been extremely costly. In August 1967, the government and the party were in disarray; the PLA was the only authoritative organization in the whole country. The only other prestigious 'institution' was Chairman Mao himself. A *coup* would have pitted these last two institutions against each other and damaged both terribly. It was therefore best to unite China under PLA control in the name of the Chairman. A secret inspection tour in late August apparently convinced Mao that this was the only sensible course.

The period that followed (1968–73) is often described as one of 'military control'. The role of the PLA was essentially one of peacekeeping, while business was conducted by civilian cadres from the discredited local party and government organs. The return to civilian control was slowed not so much by the army's unwillingness to yield power as by continued infighting in Beijing and by intramilitary cleavages. Both of these factors contributed to the fall of Lin Biao in 1971.

The Lin Biao Affair

Regional commanders dragged their feet on the rebuilding of the civilian party in 1968–72, because they did not dare to let Lin Biao and the radicals around Jian Qing control the rebuilt party. The radical's first move surely would be to purge the regional commands. Lin and Jiang Qing had misbehaved too capriciously in 1967 to risk civil chaos again. So, although everyone wanted to rebuild the party, no one was in any hurry because political opponents would control significant parts of it. Something or somebody had to give before rebuilding could proceed.

Inevitably, the impasse worked against Lin, Mao's designated successor and Deputy Chairman. Some MR commanders increased the pressure by independently forming provincial party committees which Beijing did not control. Lin's jealousy of his newly won power also displeased Mao. In November 1969, Mao's criticism of the PLA escalated. His turn back toward order and moderation found expression in his criticism of the idea that politics was everything while workstyle was secondary, a notion by now closely associated with Lin Biao.

As Mao and the political centre of gravity moved to the right, Lin remained behind in a vulnerable 'ultra-leftist' position. His power base was so narrow that he could not match Mao's shift back toward moderation. Yet Lin's acquiescence in the ruthless suppression of the Red Guards had weakened the radicals around Jiang Qing. After that betrayal, Lin could not count on the backing of the radicals either.

Lin had also become identified with China's international

belligerence, and a notion of 'self-reliance' that rejected foreign trade and models. By 1970, it was evident that that policy condemned China to political isolation, economic stagnation, and military weakness. In August 1971, *Hong Qi* said those opposing Mao's opening to the United States were guilty of 'subjectivism, dogmatism, and idealism', all deviations later attributed to Lin.

Lin's support came from his personal following in the navy, the air force, the General Logistics Department (GLD), and a few MR leaders. He could retain the support of the Central Committee radicals only so long as he retained the chairman's personal backing. Arrayed against him was a solidifying coalition of civilian and military moderates, which included most of the MR commanders. The base of support was so narrow and Lin's foes so many, that the withdrawal of the Chairman's personal support would be disastrous. Mao's support was never unconditional, so Lin was forced to try all possible means to buttress his position. Yet, every move he made to consolidate his power increased Mao's suspicion. This vicious circle led to Lin's downfall. In September 1971 he allegedly attempted a *coup d'état*, and then died attempting to flee by air toward the Soviet Union.

Zhou versus the 'Gang'

From Lin Biao's disappearance to Mao's death in 1976, PRC politics revolved around conflict between the radical group surrounding Jiang Qing (afterwards called the 'Gang of Four') and moderates led by Zhou Enlai. In September 1973, the national press, under the auspices of the 'Gang of Four', published calls to 'learn from Shanghai in militia building'. Model militia units in Shanghai reportedly trained without PLA involvement, and were solely responsible to the local civilian party. The radicals even attempted to create a National Militia Command directly responsible to themselves.[15] While paying lip service to 'learning from Shanghai', regional commanders retained control of militia units and weapons. The 'Gang' allegedly planned a *coup d'état*, and supposedly attempted one in October 1976, but it failed, even in Shanghai.

In late 1973 and early 1974, eight of the eleven MR commanders were reassigned. Six had been doubling as heads of provincial party committees, but all gave these posts up. That these powerful commanders obediently allowed themselves to be reshuffled demonstrated that they were not bent on retaining civil power. They had been worried about renewed radicalism, but had been reassured by the return of domestic order and moderate foreign policy, by the purge of Lin Biao, and by the weakening of Jiang Qing's group. They were especially reassured by the rehabili-tation of Deng Xiaoping (May 1973) and numerous purged PLA cadres, and by the appointment of Marshal Ye Jianying as MND.[16]

At the 4th National People's Congress in January 1975, Deng Xiaoping became PLA Chief of Staff. In August Luo Ruiqing reappeared, virtually completing the rehabilitation of PLA men. However, a dispute over economic priorities developed among the moderates. The 'steel versus electronics' debate was over the decision to de-emphasize military research and development in favour of agriculture and capital construction. Exploiting the dispute, the radicals made one last attempt at radicalizing the PLA. Zhang Chunqiao, one of the 'Gang of Four', became Director of the GPD. He launched a campaign against 'bourgeois right', singling out military rank as its most harmful manifestation in the army. He imposed another *xialian* movement much like the one in 1958.

By mid-1975, the PLA had effectively returned to the barracks. Top military leaders were still involved in infighting in the Central Committee, but that was (and is) inherent in any Leninist regime. Particularly among the 'old warriors' of the first revolutionary generation, the 'military-civilian' distinction simply was not applicable. But the PLA as an institution had withdrawn from domestic administration and police work. The authority of the party over the army had survived a severe test. Through the experience, attempts to radicalize the officer corps had met formal obedience and passive resistance. Officers adapted to the rhetoric of the times while maintaining a deep conservatism.

Mao's Death and 'Radical Revisionism'

Mao died in September 1976. Senior PLA men, notably Ye Jianying, Nie Rongzhen, and Xu Shiyou, played instrumental roles in the arrest of the 'Gang of Four' in early October. For the next four years, the leading triumvirate was Hua Guofeng, Deng Xiaoping, and Ye Jianying, with Ye frequently appearing to arbitrate between the other two. As Deng resumed his efforts to professionalize and reform the PLA, he also strengthened his political hand against Hua Guofeng and the 'restorationists'.[17]

Whereas the PLA high command was considerably to the 'right' of the political mainstream during the Cultural Revolution, senior officers emphasized many 'leftist' aspects of the revolutionary tradition in 1977–86. Theirs was a fairly consistent stance, tending toward moderation, balancing modernization and expertise with people's war and political work. They advocated a 'red and expert' balance because the Chinese people, especially mid-level cadres, would fear retribution as long as the party line continued to oscillate violently. Even more fundamentally, the old revolutionary faith was not to be cast aside until new myths and symbols replaced the old ones.

The PLA's 'old warriors' sought to dampen what they saw as extremism in rapid change and modernization. Throughout 1978–79, senior military leaders went against the 'revisionist' tide, publicly advocating policies which sounded 'Maoist', or at least comparatively 'revolutionary' in the traditional sense.[18] New PLA political work regulations were promulgated in August 1978 which differed little from Lin Biao's regulations of 1963, except for references to the villainous Lin Biao and the anarchical 'Gang of Four'. As far as the 'old warriors' were concerned, politics and expertise were still equally important. The leading role of the unit party committees, the commissar system, and the class brotherhood of officers and men were all reiterated. The air force's First Flight Division became a model, making the point that traditional political work was possible in a high-technology setting. In August 1978, draft 'Regulations on the Service of Officers of the PLA' were ratified, but never released. Evidently, the regulations were still controversial. It appears the PLA was on the verge of reintroducing a rank system in 1978, until several senior officers publicly objected. In sharp contrast to the growing élitism in the rest of the society, the MAC again ordered 'going down to the companies' in August 1978—the last time *xiafang* was practised anywhere in China.

The surviving 'old warriors' of the PLA high command have been 'conservatives' right through the 1980s. A 'conservative' is one who defends the myths, symbols, and traditions of his society against rapid or destabilizing change. The old soldiers were not opposed to change, *per se*. On the contrary, they were vitally concerned with technological progress and understood the importance of a stable society for military preparedness. Accordingly, they resisted excessive zeal which they saw threatening social, political and economic stability. In contrast, many younger military officers have seemed ready to discard 'politicization' altogether. These younger officers, recruited after about 1945, lack the 'old warriors'' revolutionary experience and perhaps their military-political breadth of vision. Their battle experiences have been relatively modern and conventional, in Korea, India, and Vietnam; they lack personal experience with 'people's war'. They have no wish to repeat their only experience with political power during the chaos of the 'Great Leap Forward' and the 'Cultural Revolution'. Already in 1977–78, they were pressing for full-scale modernization and reform. Since these younger men strongly support Deng Xiaoping's policies, Deng's primary problem in reforming the PLA has been to place them in commanding positions, replacing the 'old warriors'.

Reform: 1972–89

The PLA's transition from its light infantry past toward a modern combined-arms future resumed when Deng Xiaoping was 'rehabilitated' and named Chief of Staff. At a meeting of the MAC in May 1975, Deng called for the revival of military colleges and academies,[19] saying that only formal military schools could produce professional officers capable of defending China.[20] Deng's reforms were delayed by the dramatic events of 1976, but in August 1977 he was 'rehabilitated' again and resumed his efforts.

Reform was spurred by the PLA's poor showing in its 1979 incursion into Vietnam.[21] 'Maoist' tactics caused excessive casualties. Cadres at all levels were unable to control dispersed forces and employ supporting arms, especially artillery.[22] A 1978 Conference on Military Academies initiated major improvements in all aspects of personnel qualification, training, and education.[23] In 1982, training emphasis officially shifted from individual soldiers to cadres.[24] The national strategy of 'people's war under modern conditions[25] emerged, which required comprehensive modernization of tactics, organization, logistics, weapons, and equipment, as well as training.[26]

The announced defence budget for 1988 was Rmb 21.53 billion ($5.78 billion). Since 1980, defence budgets have been in the Rmb 18–21 billion range, but have dropped from over six per cent of GNP to less than three per cent.[27] Military leaders stated in 1986 that the objective likelihood of a major war has been so reduced by United States–Soviet nuclear stalemate that the world faces a 'relatively long period of stability and peace'. The PLA therefore made a 'strategic change of ideology' from readiness for an 'early war, major war, and nuclear war' to a long period of building a 'regularized modern, revolutionary army'.[28] Despite its low economic priority, the PLA has achieved much relatively inexpensive modernization.

In the early 1980s, owing to a combination of neglect and the decentralized guerrilla tradition, some cadres did not understand even the rudiments of their profession. A cadre typically served his entire career in the same regiment, with little standardized training, and no rotation to other units or places.[29] Unit procedures varied so widely as to make coordinated operations nearly impossible. 'Regularization' (*zhenggui hua*), therefore, required more than modernized technology and changed tactics. It required standardized procedures, rationalized organization, and tightened discipline to end old decentralized, semi-autonomous, self-sufficient 'guerrilla war habits'.[30]

Reorganization has eliminated the field artillery, armour, railroad troops, combat engineers, and Capital Construction Engineer Corps (CCEC) branches. All were either transferred to civilian management or downgraded to sub-departments of the GSD. In 1984, the Strategic Rocket Force (*Zhanlue Huojian Budui*) was created, taking over most of the missions of the former Second Artillery Corps. In June 1985, the state council directed consolidation of the Military Regions (MRs), from eleven to seven, facilitating regional defence and enhancing the authority of the MR commanders. It also ordered a one-million men reduction in PLA strength.

Through the 1980s, the PLA has divested itself of nonmilitary functions such as construction and police work. Many local force (*difang bingtuan*) units have transferred to the People's Armed Police Force (PAPF) which is subordinate to the Ministry of Public Security. As with the CCEC and the railroad troops, however, PAPF troops are still recruited through the national conscription system, and influenced by PLA political work.

The People's Armed Forces Departments, which are the lowest level command organs of the People's Militia, were ordered to revert from military to civilian governmental control in 1985. This process has proceeded slowly.[31] Similarly, the military rank system, mandated by the Military Service Law of 1984,[32] was not implemented until 1 October 1988. When state directives take so long to implement, it usually indicates low-level bureaucratic resistance, and possibly disagreement among the national élite.

Reorganization and Deployment

The PRC Constitution of 1982 established the State Central Military Commission (CMC; *Guojia Zhongyang Junshi Weiyuanhui*), which was supposed to take supreme command of the armed forces, replacing the party's MAC. In 1983–87 the State CMC was seldom mentioned, while the MAC remained the ultimate locus of military control. The state and party commissions evidently had identical membership, and the press usually referred to the 'Central Military Commission (*Zhong Jun Hui*)', an abbreviation routinely applied to the MAC before 1982—thus muddling whether the referent was the state or the party organ. In November 1987, the 13th Party Congress reasserted the pre-eminence of the State CMC, and a few members of that body have subsequently been identified who are not known to be on the MAC. Nevertheless, there remain two theoretically separate organs with nearly identical memberships and identical functions. The most probable explanation is continuing disagreement, at the highest level, over the momentous question of whether the PLA serves the state or the party.[33]

In 1984–86 PLA reserve division and regiments were 'officially included in the PLA organizational system and given designations and colors'.[34] Like Soviet reserve units, they have 'soldiers on active duty as their mainstay and officers and men on reserve [i.e., part-time] duty as their foundation. . . . They can quickly turn into active-duty forces . . . when needed'.[35] Peng Dehuai's dream of a regular PLA reserve may be realized at last.

The most significant reorganization in 1985–86 was conversion of all mainforce Corps (*Zhuli Jun*; also called field armies: *Ye Jun*) into Group Armies (*Jituan Jun*). Like the old Corps, Group Armies vary in size and organization. One of the most technically advanced appears to be the former 38th Corps, stationed near Beijing, which is a 'Mechanized Group Army'. It has infantry and artillery units as well as armoured, signal, chemical warfare, engineering and air defence units, plus a flight unit (presumably helicopters), and an electronic warfare unit.[36] The percentage of infantrymen has declined to roughly 20 per cent within this Group Army.

This Mechanized Group Army is evidently structured like a Soviet Combined Arms Army, a fully mechanized formation in which even the constituent manoeuvre divisions and regiments are fully-integrated combined arms units. It is unlikely that any PLA Group Army is fully mechanized yet, or has achieved extensive integration of arms. Such is clearly the intent, however, for by the early 1987 there were reports of reorganization along these lines in Chinese divisions and even regiments.

The mission of the Mechanized Group Armies will be to conduct the 'mobile defence' phase of 'People's War Under Modern Conditions', meeting Soviet forces in mechanized manoeuvre warfare.[37] This capability is still years away, however, owing to high cost and technological lag. For the foreseeable future, the PLA is more likely to fight small clashes along the southern borders than all-out war with the Russians. In 1987–89 the PLA press raised the issue of 'local wars' and the special troops needed for them. Military officers and civilians debated the lessons of recent wars in the Middle East, the Falklands, Vietnam, etc. 'Rapid-deployment forces' were said to be crucial in such conflicts, and in 1988 an experimental battalion-sized force was formed to develop the concept.[38]

Education and Training

Expansion and reorganization of military education and training continues, affecting everything from basic training to the education of generals. In January 1986, the PLA National Defense

University (NDU) opened. It combines the former Higher Military and Political Academies and Logistics Academy. It includes a research department which functions as a defence 'think tank'. NDU's first students included some civilian officials—the first civilians to enroll in a PLA academy since 1949. NDU will 'enhance the leading officials' capacity in making macroscopic *political* decisions'.[39] The perceived need for this is symptomatic of the passing of the older generation of military-political revolutionary cadres.

In 1983 the annual Conference on Military Academies and Schools decided that formal professional education should receive top priority, 'even if it means fewer soldiers and manning offices with fewer people'.[40] Instructors are to rotate between schools and operational units, as in most modern armies. In 1986, Vice-Premier (now Premier) Li Peng told the conference that PLA education must adopt an 'open policy' to 'assimilate the latest achievements in the world's military science and technology . . .' Foreign students now attend PLA schools. There are foreign speakers and even visiting faculty.[41]

Each Group Army must establish a basic-training regiment, which will conduct standardized recruit training. As in the Soviet Army, selected recruits will then be sent on to an NCO academy prior to joining operational units.[42] In 1986, the Combined Arms Tactical Training Centre opened in the Nanjing MR, modelled on the American National Training Center at Ft. Irwin, California. It has facilities for heavy weapons firing and electronic warfare training, and the capacity to conduct 10–15 division-sized exercises each year.[43] The sporadic fighting along the Vietnamese border is utilized for its 'training value' as units from all over China are rotated to the battle zone.

Officer acquisition is being regularized in entry-level officer academies. Over 9,000 graduates of senior middle schools enrolled in these academies in 1986. They received a college education plus military training prior to entering the PLA as officers. In addition, a system similar to American ROTC began operating at 69 civilian universities and colleges in 1986.[44] There are specialized technical pre-commissioning schools such as the National Defense Electronics University in Hefei, the navy submarine school in Qingdao and the various flight schools. All pilots and some maintenance personnel supposedly are learning English.

Besides formal schools, the PLA sponsors various types of 'mass education'. It publishes a variety of educational materials[45] and operates massive programmes of 'part-time education'. In 1985, 2.5 million PLA men were reportedly involved in such programmes, including 142,000 taking university or college courses.[46] It is difficult to tell how much real education has taken place, because statistics seem intentionally vague.[47]

The PLA is short of funds, facilities, and qualified instructors. While the decision to start rotating instructors between academies and operational units will enhance faculty quality in the long run, it exacerbates the current shortage. The PLA is constantly admonished to economize and conserve. While this has prompted increased efficiency, there is also a tendency to 'eliminate waste' by over-planning and over-supervising.[48] The Chinese have recognized the cost-effectiveness of computerized simulation, which has been widely applied in all services. Allotted training time varies, though it is increasingly devoted to military (as opposed to political or 'cultural') training.[49]

Chinese strategic doctrine is being rethought in the new research institutes of the PLA and various civilian institutions.[50] In March 1986, the PLA's Academy of Military Science, which virtually monopolized 'strategic research' until recently, hosted a Symposium on the Study of Military Theory. Chief of Staff Yang Dezhi stated, 'It is necessary to . . . give full play to the role of the strategic researchers, instead of relying on the efforts of the policy makers alone'.[51]

The 11th All-PLA Conference on Military Academies (October 1980) promulgated detailed Professional Military Education requirements for cadre promotion.[52] Appended, however, was the caveat that 'the majority of commanding cadres at and above battalion level have not received academy education. Therefore, when it is time to promote regimental and corps-level cadres, interim procedures may be adopted, until 1985, when the system of posts corresponding with diplomas will be fully implemented.' There was no announcement in 1985, which indicates the goals were not met. After all, the ground forces cadres of 1980 were overwhelmingly of peasant origin, many with less than junior middle school education.[53] Nevertheless, the overall level has risen considerably. The air force, navy, and rocket forces have probably met the 1980 standards.

Formally, military education is now a requirement for promotion. But who decides whether an individual has fulfilled the requirements? What assurance is there that the unit party committee, political commissar, and commander will give preference to persons with proper education as opposed to those with personal connections (*guanxi*)? The historic PLA problem of 'red versus expert' may be replaced by a new '*guanxi* versus expert' dichotomy.[54]

Personnel

Getting rid of old cadres was vital because some of them stubbornly resisted reform. 'Some people' even questioned whether soldiers needed to learn science and technology. Some were physically frail or even senile. A variety of strategies, persistently applied in 1978–88, gradually created room for the promotion of younger and better-educated men. Supposedly, promotion will hereafter be based on 'regular' qualifications, rather than 'the decadent concept of appointing people to posts [solely] according to seniority'.[55]

For millennia, Chinese governments have been plagued by the social and economic impact of demobilized soldiers. Since about 1983, soldiers have been attending classes to learn civilian skills. This effort to train people 'good at two things' (*liangyong rencai*) is meant to smooth the transition to civilian society.[56]

Many countries use their armies as schools for citizenship and to provide non-military occupational training. The practice became politically charged in China because so many high-ranking cadres were forced to retire. In 1985–87, the GSD was reportedly 'halved'. 'Some demobilized cadres are believed to still enjoy their former salaries, housing, and other perquisites.'[57]

The million-men reduction still leaves the PLA at about 3.5 million—the world's second largest military force. The reduction reportedly cut the officer corps by 25 per cent, thereby reducing the 'irrational ratio between officers and men'. Seventy-six officer positions were reclassified as enlisted men's jobs.[58] Finally, late in 1988, about 80,000 non-combatant cadres were 'civilianized'. These included technical and administrative personnel ranging from filing clerks to research scientists. Commentators explicitly compare them to the civilian employees of the US Defense Department, though Chinese non-military cadres seem to be more 'military'. They are treated as soldiers regarding housing, hospitalization, and leave. The system is not considered transitional, for at least some technical and scientific units intend to continue recruiting 'non-military cadres'.[59] This category of personnel is unprecedented in any Leninist army, but the Soviet army currently is considering adaption of a similar system, citing the PLA example![60]

Changes in civilian society have complicated PLA recruitment, especially of technicians and officers. Whereas China's best and brightest young people used to enter the army as a means of advancement, they now tend to avoid it. Military service reputedly reduces their ability to save money and get married.[61] Civilian sector reforms have also created glamorous new alternatives.

Foreign Military Contact and Conflict

About 1980, the PLA became the first Marxist-Leninist army to join the *Conseil International du Sport Militaire* (*CISM*), and hosted its 1982 shooting competition in Beijing.[62] Military attachés now serve in most PRC embassies. The PLA and various foreign armed forces have been trading delegations and VIP visits since about 1978. The Chinese have been cautious about the prospects of foreign, and especially American, weapons and military technology imports, and about foreign military relations generally. China cannot afford to buy all it needs, nor could it depend on imported weapons in a crisis, so while it buys technology and a few weapon systems, it must depend primarily on itself.[63]

A British flotilla made the first western naval port call at Shanghai in 1980. By 1986, port calls were made by the Italian, British, United States, and Dutch navies. In addition to 'friendship', all of them were interested in showing military technology which they hoped to sell to China. In late 1985 a small Chinese flotilla made port calls in Pakistan, Sri Lanka, and Bangladesh. On the return voyage, it encountered elements of the US Seventh

Fleet. According to the US Navy, they 'conducted a passing exercise'. PRC diplomatic sources emphatically denied there had been any sort of joint 'exercise', saying they only 'exchanged greetings'. These differing versions are symptomatic of the Sino-American military relationship in the late 1980s: Americans emphasize the positive while Chinese play down the connection. There has been no information from either government, of course, on perhaps the most important area of cooperation: since the late 1970s, rumours have circulated about American-run intelligence facilities monitoring the Soviet Union from western China.

China has had close military contacts with Pakistan and North Korea for decades. Since 1971, the PLA has established relations with the armies of many African, Middle Eastern and South Asian states as well. The Chinese and Romanian armies and defence industries have collaborated since the 1960s. The Chinese are currently working to establish ties with Latin American and Southeast Asian armies.

China continues to provide military support to the Khmer Rouge, and began providing military aid to non-communist Khmer resistance factions in 1985. The Sino-Vietnamese border conflict has simmered since 1979, usually escalating in January–February. The heaviest fighting was on 3–8 January 1987, when the Chinese claimed 500 Vietnamese killed, while the Vietnamese claimed 1,500 Chinese killed or seriously wounded. The Chinese instigate most of these battles in response to events in Cambodia. Reported clashes have been fewer and smaller since Vietnam began substantial troop withdrawals from Cambodia in mid-1987.

Arms Transfers

Since 1978, China has become a major arms exporter, ranking fifth in the world in 1988. The main customers in 1981–88 were Iraq and Iran. Arms sales are the source of foreign exchange for military industry, and an important sector of PRC foreign trade. NORINCO, then the export arm of the Ordnance Ministry, was reportedly China's fifth leading exporter in 1985, with sales of $1.5 billion. This sum did not include sales of ships, aircraft, etc., by other ministries. In 1986–89 China delivered artillery and armoured vehicles to Thailand. The immediate aim is political support against Vietnam, but the Chinese hope eventually to break into the Southeast Asian arms market. Faced with the region's traditional suspicion of China, they have met little success so far.

In 1984, China's defence industries began exhibiting their wares at international exhibitions. They have hosted several exhibitions, notably the NATSEDES exhibitions in Shanghai (1983 and 1989) and the ASIANDEX exhibitions in Beijing (1986 and 1988). While one aim of arms exhibitions is to sell Chinese equipment, another is to facilitate technology imports. The Chinese are marketing a 155 mm gun of Austrian design, and prototype joint-venture armoured vehicles that feature Chinese chassis with foreign turrets. They are co-producing French Dauphin-II helicopters and American Motors Jeeps. British avionics are included in their principal export-version fighter–interceptor, and there are components from Israel, Italy, and France in other Chinese weapons systems.

Americans have been negotiating arms sales to China since at least 1982, with few results, mainly for financial reasons. The United States government agrees in principle to allow the sale of arms and arms technologies to China in four ('defensive') 'mission areas': anti-tank, anti-aircraft, anti-submarine, and field artillery. 1986 saw the first export of lethal American military technology: technical assistance in Chinese production of large-calibre artillery shells. In 1987, the United States agreed to assist in up-grading avionics in the F-8II fighter.

Defence Industry and Weapons Developments

The national organs that oversee the defence industry have been reorganized repeatedly since 1981–82. Currently, the ministerial-level Commission on Science, Technology and Industry for National Defence (COSTIND) has overall responsibility, including integration with the civilian sector. Defence industrial ministries have been reorganized and consolidated repeatedly, at least partly owing to bureaucratic politics. As in the civilian sector, small, inefficient factories have been closed, while others have been consolidated. Management in military factories is supposed to be reorganized according to the 'responsibility system'. Workers, party committees and cadres have resisted, if anything, more stoutly than their civilian counterparts.

Chinese weapons systems and factories are being improved incrementally as technology, capital, and qualified personnel become available. Military plants and laboratories were underutilized for decades. Reorganization is partly intended to apply them to civilian use (tractors from tank factories, for example). Military production for export, however, is more prestigious and profitable. It is not clear what portion of export earnings gets back to defence industry for reinvestment.

Combat Forces

Nearly all the 4,600 or so fighter–interceptors of the PLA air force and navy are effective only in daylight and clear weather. Since they are tightly controlled from the ground, fighters are further limited by poor radar coverage and the vulnerability of radar and communications to electronic counter-measures. The Chinese hope to equip their air force with the American-updated F-8II 'around the year 2000'.[64]

Though substantially reduced, PLA ground forces still have two million men and perhaps 12,000 tanks, organized in some one hundred main-force divisions, plus local forces. Ground forces still have glaring vulnerabilities; anti-tank defence, air defence, chemical-biological defence, and logistics, to name a few.

While the navy remains primarily a coastal defence force, it now has a modest 'blue water' capability. Since 1982, the force of *Jianghu*-class missile frigates has grown from 10 to 22. Eighty coastal and non-combatant vessels were de-activated during 1986, while a new destroyer class is said to be under development.[65] Coastal defences continue to rely heavily on diesel-electric submarines, mostly copies of the Soviet *Romeo* class. There are supposedly three *Han*-class nuclear attack submarines as well. Both types are armed with unguided torpedoes and have other shortcomings, although the *Hans* have reportedly been fitted with French sonars.[66] Current naval construction plans call for modernization of at least two-thirds of the *Romeos*, in addition to new classes of diesel-electric and nuclear attack submarines by 1991. The experimental *Wuhan*-class is a *Romeo*, converted to surface-launch six C-801 missiles.[67] The Chinese are reportedly seeking European and American bids for submarine technology, systems management and training.[68]

A priority for the submarine and surface fleets is anti-submarine warfare (ASW), long the Achilles heel of the PLA navy. The new frigates are intended for ASW missions, as are the navy's western helicopters. Anti-surface ship weapons include the ground-launched SILKWORM (a modified Soviet STYX), and possible ground- and air-launched versions of the C-801.[69]

The nuclear missile programme still enjoys high national priority, but progress is slow. Multiple independently targeted re-entry vehicles (MIRV) and tactical nuclear weapons are probably in advanced development. China began offering space launch services to the outside world in 1986, utilizing CSL-2 and CSL-3 rockets, which are modifications of the CSS-4 ICBM. A submarine-launched ballistic missile, the CSS-NX-3, made a successful submerged launch in October 1982. In January 1987, the *People's Daily* announced that the first *Xia*-class nuclear ballistic missile submarine was operational. Its missiles and command-and-control systems are probably not yet fully operational, however. A handful of long-range CSS-3 and CSS-4 missiles are deployed in mountain caves and silos. Dispersion and concealment, plus the mobility of shorter-range missiles, make a successful preemptive 'first strike' against China unlikely.

Civil-Military Relations

Continuing the post-Cultural Revolution trend, civil-military relations have been stable, but interesting, since Mao's death. Some PLA 'old warriors' have opposed reform, because they found their positions threatened by reorganization, their beliefs challenged by new policies, and their experience rendered irrelevant by modernization. They were largely displaced in the top commands in 1982–88 by much younger, more professional, better educated and less politically active officers. Routine demobilization and the large-scale personnel reductions in 1985–87 further reduced resistance.

Five military aircraft defected to Taiwan or South Korea in

1982–1987, indicating cynicism and sagging morale in the PLA. As China has liberalized and decentralized its economy, nepotism, influence peddling, and profiteering have become more visible in the PLA, as in the rest of society. A particularly pernicious effect of the Cultural Revolution was to create in PLA cadres a sense that they were a privileged class above the law. In January 1986, Yang Dezhi said, 'We not only need law to govern our country, we also need law to govern our army.'[70] In 1986 some high-ranking officers and their relatives got involved in foreign arms sales, even setting up export firms which competed with state organs. Such 'bureaucratic racketeering' has become sufficiently widespread in the army that it is a specific target of disciplinary action and political rectification.

Formal party rectification in the PLA continued from 1983 into 1986.[71] In the late 1970s 50 to 80 per cent of some military units were party members. In June 1981, the MAC directed a reduction to no more than 20 per cent. Therefore, a large proportion of the 1985–87 manpower cuts probably involved party members.[72] While the upper levels of the GPD have been manned by reformers, lower level commissars have repeatedly been criticized for arrogance, ineffectiveness, and ossified political attitudes. This has been part cause and part effect of commissar roles being reduced by reforms.

An enlarged CMC meeting in December 1986, attended by MR and Group Army commanders, emphasized that the army should 'establish the modernization programme as the main task'.[73] On 25 February 1987, the Party Central Committee announced a CMC 'Decision on Armed Forces Political Work in the New Period' which states that 'all work of the armed forces should be aimed at enhancing their fighting capabilities'.[74] It specified a system of political officers, party committees, and political work organs similar to those specified in Lin Biao's 1963 Political Work Regulations. Now, however, the cardinal indicators of a soldier's 'ideological' correctness are professional competence and obedience (defined as 'adherence to the Party's line, principles and policies').

National leaders have thus adopted an approach which 'seeks to make technological values the basis for ideological and political correctness'.[75] Contradicting Mao's concept of 'politics in command', political work now supports command authority and technical modernization. As Zhang Siye, Vice-President of the PLA political academy, wrote in 1984, '. . . one's political consciousness must be reflected in one's professional skill. . . . the slogan of "giving prominence to politics" is still a main obstacle. . . .'[76]

By inculcating technological values, a good start has been made in creating a system of clear civilian party control over the armed forces and inculcating professional values in the officer corps, curbing any tendency toward prætorianism. Deng currently has the situation under control, and officers generally accept the PLA's low economic priority. Little of China's recently developed military equipment appears to be in PLA service, most of it evidently going for export. In the long run, the PLA will benefit from the experience and technology acquisition associated with manufacturing these systems. For the time being, though, it must be frustrating to serve in an obsolescent army while reasonably modern weapons are being exported. If frustration persists too long, military leaders might demand a bigger share of state resources and a commensurately louder political voice.

Conclusion

The PLA's stormy passage from guerrilla force to modern army is finally beginning to reach its goals. Reorganization of the combat forces is well underway, and overall military restructuring appears to be nearly complete. PLA officers are fewer, younger, and generally reform-minded. Virtually all accept the need for technological modernization, reorganization, a revised national strategy, and 'opening' to the outside. PLA generals, however, remain an influential, if less assertive, voice in domestic cultural and political affairs. However, there is not likely to be much reversal, or even delay, in the course of military modernization and restructuring. After the setbacks imposed by Mao, Lin Biao and the 'Gang of Four', the army is back on the course charted by Peng Dehuai in the mid-1950s. The PLA, in a 'China at Forty', has become one of the most stable, and conservative institutions. At a time of great uncertainty in much of the rest of China, the PLA will be relied upon to help hold the pieces together.

1. The best study is still Allen S. Whiting, *China Crosses the Yalu* (Stanford: Stanford University Press, 1968).
2. Alexander L. George, *The Chinese Communist Army in Action*, and Samuel B. Griffith, *The Chinese People's Liberation Army* (McGraw-Hill, 1967).
3. Quoted in He Di, 'The Evolution of the People's Republic of China's Policy Toward the Offshore Islands (Quemoy, Matsu)', a paper presented to the Center for Chinese Studies Regional Seminar, 31 Oct., 1987, University of California, Berkeley. The following discussion draws heavily on He Di.
4. Alice L. Hseih, *Communist China's Strategy in the Nuclear Era* (Prentice-Hall, 1962), p. 27.
5. Translated in Ellis Joffe, *Party and Army: Professionalism and Political Control in the Chinese Officer Corps, 1949–1964*. Harvard East Asian Monographs, 1967, p. 6.
6. On the origins of the Chinese nuclear programme, see John Wilson Lewis and Xue Litai, *China Builds the Bomb* (Stanford: Stanford University Press, 1988).
7. On the nuclear power-sharing agreements, see Harvey Nelsen 'Strategic Weapons and the Sino-Soviet Dispute', *Issues and Studies*, 21, No. 11 (Nov. 1985), pp. 103–18.
8. Joffe, *Party and Army*, pp. 142–3.
9. David P. Mozingo and Thomas W. Robinson, *Lin Biao on People's War: China Takes a Second Look at Vietnam* (RAND Corporation, 1965).
10. On guardian coups, see Samuel P. Huntington, *Political Order in Changing Societies* (Yale: Yale University Press, 1968), pp. 225–6.
11. See Harlan W. Jencks, *From Muskets to Missiles*, Westview, 1982, chapter 4; Harvey Nelsen, 'Military Bureuacracy in the Cultural Revolution', *Asian Survey*, 4, no. 4 (Apr. 1974); and Harvey Nelsen, *The Chinese Military System*, (Boulder: Westview, 1977), pp. 148–9.
12. Nelsen, 'Military Bureuacracy', p. 379.
13. Nelsen, *The Chinese Military System*, pp. 148–9.
14. Jürgen Domes, 'The Role of the Military in the Formation of Revolutionary Committees', *China Quarterly*, No. 44 (Oct.–Dec. 1970), pp. 122–3 and 140–1.
15. "Failure of the 'Gang of Four's Scheme to Set Up a 'Second Armed Force'' ", *Peking Review*, No. 13 (25 March 1977), pp. 10–12.
16. For major military figures rehabilitated in 1973–4, see Jencks, *Muskets to Missiles*, pp. 116–19.
17. The term 'restorationist' is taken from Harry Harding, *China's Second Revolution: China After Mao* (Washington: Brookings, 1987).
18. For example, see the speeches at the All Army Political Work Conference, 29 May 1978, in *XH*, 4 June 1978, trans. in *FBIS-China*, No. 108, p. E13.
19. Deng Xiaoping, *Deng Xiaoping Wenxuan [Selected Works of Deng Xiaoping]* (Beijing: Renmin Chuban She, 1983), pp. 15–24.
20. *Hong Qi [Red Flag]*, 1 Nov. 1983, p. 44.
21. Harlan W. Jencks, 'China's Punitive War on Vietnam', *Asian Survey*, 19, No. 8 (Aug. 1979), pp. 801–15.
22. 'Circular of the Party Central Committee', n.d., cited in *Chung-kung Yen-chiu [Studies on Chinese Communism]*, 13, No. 9 (Sept. 1979), p. 7.
23. Xin Hua, 14 May 1978.
24. Yang Dezhi, 'On Several Questions Concerning Regularization', *Jiefangjun Bao [Liberation Army Daily*, hereafter *JFJB]*, 22 Jan. 1982, trans. in *China Daily*, 4 Feb. 1982, p. 1.

25. Harlan W. Jencks, 'People's War Under Modern Conditions: Wishful Thinking, National Suicide, or Effective Deterrent?', *China Quarterly*, No. 98 (June 1984), pp. 305–19.
26. Gerald Segal and William T. Tow (eds.), *Chinese Defense Policy* (Illinois: University of Illinois Press, 1984), passim.
27. Author's estimates based on official PRC budgets, IISS figures in *Military Balance*, and *Jane's Defence Weekly*, 30 Apr. 1988, p. 819. Since the PRC's official defence budget hides as much as it reveals, these figures are useful only for comparison.
28. *Ta Kung Pao* (Hong Kong), 16 Feb. 1986, citing *JFJB*, 16 Feb. 1986; and Deng Xiaoping, *Renmin Ribao [People's Daily, hereafter RMRB]*, 24 Apr. 1986, quoted in *Hong Chi*, No. 13, (1 July 1986), pp. 20–6, trans. in *FBIS-China* 86-144, pp. A5–A14, esp. pp. A11 and A14.
29. Jencks, *From Muskets to Missiles*, chapter 6.
30. Yang Shangkun, *Hong Qi*, No. 15 (Aug. 1982), trans. *FBIS-China*, 82-148, p. K10; and *Xin Hua*, 29 May 1982.
31. Nanning Guangxi Regional Service 14 Feb. 1987, in *FBIS-China* 87-034, p. P1.
32. *Military Service Law of the People's Republic of China*, 31 May 1984.
33. Interview of Premier Zhao Ziyang on NHK-TV (Tokyo), 4 June 1982, in *FBIS-China* 82-109, pp. D1–D2. Zhao stated that 'The army is an important component of the state'.
34. Nanjing Jiangsu Prov. Svc., 11 Sept. 1984, in *FBIS-China* 84-180, p. O2; Changsha Hunan Prov. Svc., 16 Nov. 1984, in *FBIS-China* 84-224, p. P5; and *Xin Hua Dom. Svc.*, 1 Aug. 1984, in *FBIS-China* 84-153, p. K8.
35. *Xin Hua Dom. Svc.*, 7 Sept. 1986, trans. *FBIS-China* 86-177, p. K19.
36. *Xin Hua Dom. Svc.*, 6 Sept. 1986, in *FBIS-China* 86-175, pp. K12–K13.
37. Jencks, 'People's War Under Modern Conditions'; June T. Dreyer, in *Current History*, Sept. 1985; and Tai Ming Cheung, 'Goodbye people's war', *Far Eastern Economic Review* [hereafter FEER], 1 Dec. 1988, p. 21.
38. Zhang Taiheng, 'Local Conflicts and Special Troops', *JFJB*, 14 Mar. 1986, p. 3.
39. *JFJB*, no date cited by *RMRB*, 17 May 1986 (emphasis added).
40. *Xin Hua*, 3 Mar. 1983.
41. *Wenwei Po*, 27 Feb. 1986; and *Xin Hua*, 26 Feb. 1986.
42. *RMRB*, 22 Mar. 1986; and Beijing Radio, 17 Mar. 1986.
43. *Xiandai Junshi [CONMILIT, hereafter XDJS]*, No. 7, July 1986, pp. 10–11; and *JFJB*, 13 Mar. 1986.
44. *Xin Hua* (English), 5 Sept. 1986, in *FBIS-China* 86-173, p. K4. The system also now applies to pilots: *Xin Hua Domestic Svc.*, 5 Feb. 1987, in *FBIS-China* 87-29, p. K21.
45. *Xin Hua*, 21 June 1984.
46. *RMRB*, 2 Aug. 1985; and *Yunnan Ribao*, 1 Aug. 1985.
47. *RMRB*, 28 July 1985.
48. *Xin Hua*, 14 Jan. 1982.
49. *Beijing Radio*, 21 Nov. 1982.
50. Bonnie S. Glaser and Banning N. Garrett, 'Chinese Perspectives on the Strategic Defense Initiative', *Problems of Communism*, 35, No. 2 (Mar.–Apr. 1986), pp. 28–44; and A. Doak Barnett, *The Making of Foreign Policy in China* (Boulder: Westview, 1985), pp. 119–34.
51. *RMRB*, 2 Mar. 1986; and *China Daily*, 2 Aug. 1986.
52. Tang Chi-ming, 'Military Affairs in 1980', *Chung-kung Yen-chui*, 15, No. 1 (15 Jan. 1981), pp. 71–2.

53. *Beijing Dom. Svc.*, 25 Feb. 1981.
54. William R. Heaton, 'New Trends in Professional Military Education and Training', paper presented at *China's National Security Structure: Consequences of the Second Revolution*, panel at the International Studies Assoc. Convention, Anaheim, CA, 27 Mar. 1986, p. 16.
55. *Nanfang Ribao*, 2 Nov. 1982, pp. 1 and 3.
56. *RMRB*, 26 and 31 May 1986; Beijing Radio, 28 May 1986.
57. Robert Delfs in *FEER*, 15 Jan. 1987, p. 6.
58. *Wen Wei Po*, 12 Sept. 1985, quoting *JFJB*.
59. Liu Junkong, 'The Nonmilitary Cadre System Must be Implemented. . .', *JFJB*, 5 Apr. 1988, p. 12, trans. in *JPRS-CAR* 88-023 (19 May 1988), pp. 46–7; and *Jane's Defence Weekly* [hereafter *JDW*], 6 Aug. 1988, p. 197; and 'Lanzhou Hospital. . .', *JFJB*, 4 Aug. 1988.
60. I am grateful to Michael Tsypkin for this information.
61. *Liao Wang*, Dec. 1985.
62. Paul R. Stankiewicz, 'Friendship Through Sports', *Asia-Pacific Defense Forum*, Winter 1982–83, pp. 21–8.
63. The most authoritative statement on this issue was by Defence Minister Zhang Aiping in *Hong Qi*, May 1983.
64. *XJDS*, No. 96 (Nov. 1984), p. 10; and *XDJS* No. 118 (Sept. 1986), pp. 2–3; *CSM*, 19 Nov. 1986, pp. 10–11; and *Xin Hua*, 13 Jan. 1987, in *FBIS-China* 87-009, p. K10.
65. *China Daily* (no date given), cited in *JDW*, 16 May 1987, p. 945; and Gordon Jacobs and Raymond Cheung, 'China's "Jianghu" Frigate Program', *JDW*, 21 Mar. 1987, pp. 507–9.
66. P. D. Jones and J. V. P. Goldrick, 'Far Eastern Navies', *Proceedings*, Mar. 1987, p. 66.
67. 'China's Project E5SG Submarine', *JDW*, 9 May 1987, p. 912.
68. *JDW*, 28 Feb. 1987, p. 343; and *JDW*, 16 May 1987, p. 945.
69. *JDW*, 6 Jun. 1987, p. 1113.
70. *RMRB*, 8 Jan. 1986.
71. An excellent description and analysis is Alistair I. Johnston, 'Party Rectification in the People's Liberation Army', *China Quarterly*, No. 112 (Dec. 1987), pp. 591–630.
72. Ibid., p. pp. 601–3.
73. *Xin Hua Domestic Service*, 26 Dec. 1986, in *FBIS-China* 82-249, p. K18; and *Xin Hua Domestic Service*, 25 Dec. 1986, in *FBIS-China* 82-249, pp. K13–K18.
74. All of the above is drawn from *Xin Hua Domestic Service* 25 Feb. 1987, in *FBIS-China* 87-038, pp. K3–K9.
75. Heaton, William R, 'The Defense Policy of the People's Republic of China', draft chapter prepared for *The Defense Policies of Nations*, 2nd edition. USAF Academy, 1986, pp. 11–12.
76. *Hong Qi*, 16 July 1984, p. 23.

7. Chinese Foreign Policy

GERALD SEGAL

FORTY years of Chinese foreign policy can be judged from the perspective of foreigners or the Chinese themselves. Either way, the picture is of great change, including obvious successes and deep failures. The balance sheet has come out on the positive side, but not without major problems along the way. It would be convenient to suggest some pithy principles that govern Chinese foreign and defence policy. While some have attempted to outline such generalizations, it seems increasingly clear that Chinese policy is too complex to fit into such convenient strait-jackets.[1] While there may be some broad objectives of Chinese foreign policy, for example, defence of territory or furthering international socialism, there is no route map to those ends. What is more, the objectives remain so distant that flexibility in the short term can be justified.

Instead, what can be offered is an analysis of central Chinese concerns. These problems of defence policies adopted in each area have varied over the past forty years.[2] Analysts can at most outline the nature of the problem, and assess the options. In essence, Chinese policy has been concerned with four types of issues: threats to territorial integrity; threats at the frontiers; enhancing economic prosperity; and the search for global influence. Yet the analysis cannot be complete without an understanding of the domestic context of Chinese policy.

Domestic Decision Making

At one level, the question of who makes Chinese foreign policy is simple—it is the Politburo of the Chinese Communist Party (CCP).[3] Certainly the Chinese State and Party constitutions are perfectly clear on the 'leading role' of the CCP in all areas of policy. Thus an organizational chart of foreign policy making is simple. Yet, in China, as in the similar Party structure in the Soviet Union, the actual foreign policy making is far more complex.

The complexity is derived from several sources, but three seem most crucial. First, there is no single, comprehensive set of ideals, shared by all Chinese leaders, on how to govern. Debates on policy are of course normal for any state. Second, as the CCP established the People's Republic, political conflict developed, based in part on institutional affiliation.[4] China, the mother of bureaucracy, has not escaped the parochialism of institutional politics. Third, with all these divisions, Chinese leaders also split on the basis of personal factions.[5] Chinese political culture seems especially susceptible to vicious personal factionalism. This problem is made more acute since in the generation that made the revolution, the men in charge tended to hold more than one position, thus confusing lines of power and policy. Does a military professional in charge of a machine building industry act in the interests of his faction, his ministry, or the military?

Even as the CCP was consolidating power in 1949, its foreign policy was far from clear cut. Some elements of the CCP, perhaps even including Zhou Enlai, did not see an inevitable need to 'lean to the Soviet side' in the cold war. That Mao eventually led China into the Soviet camp, is as much to do with China's lack of options, as a positive desire to support the Soviet Union. The central point is that foreign policy options were seriously considered.

Later in the 1950s, when the Soviet model was called into question in China, debates returned. Did China need to rely on Moscow, or could it afford to strike out on a more independent path? The debate was protracted, cutting across almost all sectors of Chinese society. The Soviet model had penetrated so far into Chinese politics that its rejection could not have been anything but difficult. The repudiation of Soviet guidance in internal Chinese politics came first, followed by an interregnum in the early 1960s, and finally an open split on foreign policy in 1963. But all these steps were far from unanimous. In 1966 when Party-to-Party ties were severed, the debate flared once again. The factional lines were complex, linking in with the Cultural Revolution and a strategic assessment of the threat posed by the United States in the expanding Vietnam war.

With the winding up of the extreme phases of the Cultural Revolution in 1969, the pressing Soviet threat along the frontier, and the signs of detente from the United States, foreign policy again came under debate in China. The purge of Defence Minister Lin Biao in 1971 obviously was more related to domestic politics, but his opposition to the Sino-American detente was not unimportant in the formation of the anti-Lin coalition.

Debates simmered through the 1970s as radicals and moderates fought each other in anticipation of the succession to Mao Zedong. Once again, foreign policy was not the *prime* issue at stake, but it was an issue. The extent to which China's door should be open to foreign influences was a hotly debated topic. Even after the fall of the 'Gang of Four', foreign policy has continued to figure in leadership debates. The recent detente with the Soviet Union was at the centre of a strategic debate in the early 1980s. Related issues included concern over the impact of western 'spiritual pollution' and whether excessive concessions had been made to the United States over Taiwan.

Are there any patterns to these debates? It seems not. There are certain themes that recur, although the conclusions reached in the debates are not consistent. For example, there seems to be regular debate on how open China should be to foreign influences.[6] Both the Soviet model, and the late 1970s' opening to the West, were examples of receptiveness to foreign ideas. Yet the Cultural Revolution and the early 1970s are examples of xenophobia and a narrow nationalistic approach. That the open door swings to and fro is clear, but there seems to be no 'natural' place for it to be propped open or slammed shut.

Similarly, there seems to be no consensus on whether to be more concerned with the threat from the north, or with regaining Taiwan and fending off capitalist ideas. Both the Soviet and western options have advantages and disadvantages for China. One emphasizes the socialist nature of the Chinese revolution and the irreconcilable contradictions with capitalism. The other points to the looming Soviet threat to the north, and/or its ideological challenge of 'revisionism'. Whatever the case, there is no natural answer to these questions for China, and debates will continue.

There is also a fairly consistent Chinese concern with trends in international politics and the threats or opportunities posed for China. Yet the implications of this globalism are unclear. Does it lead to an interventionist Chinese policy, spreading foreign aid and offering advice on revolution or how to challenge the superpowers? Or does China retreat inward, calculating that the best way to ensure long-term strength against international problems is to develop first a strong China? And even if the latter option is chosen, is spending on the armed forces a primary part of building strength, or is the military forced to wait for general economic growth before it can get its toys? This 'guns *v.* butter' argument, as with the others, has no answer. China, like most great powers, seeks both, with the balance regularly shifting.

These, and indeed other, dilemmas of policy are at the root of foreign policy debates. The specific policies adopted result from a complex web of factors. Personal factional lines cut across ideological debates and institutional politics. Different generations may also share the views of some, but not of others. There are those trained under the Soviet model who both have a vested interest in Soviet organizational routines, but who may also loathe Russians on a personal level. There are those of the 'lost generation' of the Cultural Revolution trained to reject things foreign, who may feel alienated from a policy that encourages learning from 'advanced western technology'.

In sum, the domestic dimension of Chinese foreign policy is crucial. Policy is constantly affected by debates and natural dilemmas over options. None of these problems will diminish in importance in the near future. Neither will some of the essential realities of Chinese domestic politics that help shape foreign policy. The poverty of China forces Beijing to choose between more limited options than those faced by other great powers.

Foreign Policy Objectives

China, like most great powers, has four types of foreign policy concern. The scope and relevance of all four are often different for each great power. What is more, the relative importance of each aspect has changed in the past forty years, and certainly the policies adopted in each case have not been consistent. Thus while it is impossible to speak of principles of Chinese foreign policy, it is possible to discuss certain problems as being of enduring importance.

Territorial Integrity

China is unique among contemporary great powers in having unresolved problems of territorial integrity. While the Soviet Union has territorial claims against it (from Japan) and Britain has a secessionist movement in Northern Ireland, no great power faces China's problem of territorial claims against neighbouring states. The importance of unfinished national unification cannot be overestimated.

One primary strength of the CCP, in its triumph over the Guomindang, was its credible claim to be able to unite the state and expel foreign influence. The experience of the rape of the Qing dynasty China by imperial powers shaped the perspective of those revolutionaries who fought for power after China's 1911 revolution. While the Soviet Union may have been invaded from time to time from Western Europe, the invasions were always short-lived. In China's case, imperial occupation was measured in centuries.

If all this foreign exploitation had been terminated by the Chinese revolution in the twentieth century, then the super-sensitivity might have begun to fade. But the implications of foreign occupation are still felt today. China retains a number of problems of incomplete territorial integrity that play a major role in contemporary foreign policy.

First, there is the problem of Taiwan and the associated offshore islands. After 1949 it was plain that the CCP held *de facto* control, but the Guomindang was able to maintain the fiction of its claim in large part because the Chinese civil war was also an international event. With the United States having supported the Guomindang, and the CCP being associated with the communist bloc in the cold war, the division of China coincided with the division of international politics.

The CCP's revolutionary experience was, however, not dependent on its international communist links. Like Tito in Yugoslavia, but on a grander scale, the CCP came to power on its own. Therefore, there was a natural Chinese pride in its special revolution, and its greater relevance to other Third World states. Yet in part the validity of the Chinese claim to international stature depended upon its ability to show that its revolution was not partial, and could overcome all problems left over by the colonial legacy. Therefore, the unresolved Taiwan problem appeared all the more galling to the CCP leadership.

The fact that Taiwan was supported by the United States, and the mainland was communist, soon gave a cold war feel to the Taiwan problem. Questions of Chinese territorial integrity seemed overtaken by larger events. Yet until the outbreak of the Korean War in June 1950, globalization of the Taiwan problem was by no means inevitable.

The Korean War and the decision by President Truman to have the United States Seventh Fleet patrol the Taiwan Straits ensured that American involvement in the Chinese civil war would continue. It also meant that the CCP had to put off its planned assault on Taiwan. The process of national unification was then in its final stages with the capture of Tibet and Hainan island in 1950. However, the CCP's limited capability, especially in amphibious operations, could not overcome American military power.

The Korean war not only resulted in a new role for the Seventh Fleet but also necessitated a Chinese military operation. The collapse of the North Korean drive, and the American counter-offensive up to the Yalu river bordering on China, drew a Chinese counter-punch in October 1950.[7] Now the notion of a full-scale invasion of Taiwan was clearly out of the question. PLA arms were being used in direct support of an ally in trouble. It was made even more necessary by the fact that the United States had directly intervened in the Chinese civil war and thus constituted China's main foreign threat. The PLA operation in Korea was undoubtedly costly, but the risks of inaction were perceived as greater, both for China's security and for its sense of national pride.

With the winding down of the Korean War, China turned once again to consideration of the territorial problem and Taiwan. The first Taiwan Straits crisis in 1954–5 was in part a Chinese probe to determine the United States and Taiwanese position. China had regained some minor offshore islands since 1949, but such larger islands as Quemoy and Matsu in the Taiwan Straits posed special problems.

The Chinese probe of Taiwan's intentions in the 1954–5 crisis was also a test of American intentions as the United States built up alliances in East Asia. The establishment of the Southeast

Asian Treaty Organization (SEATO) was clearly a prime purpose behind the Chinese challenge. As a result of this first Taiwan crisis, China learned that the United States was prepared to prevent the loss of territory to the communists. China also learned that its forces were unable and, more to the point, unwilling to run great risks to take the offshore islands. Therefore it was even less likely that China could launch an operation against the main island of Taiwan. This recognition of the realities of power was hard for Beijing to acknowledge.

The second Taiwan Straits crisis in 1958 was similar. The United States made it clear that it was not prepared to tolerate Chinese territorial gains, and Taiwan once again proved its ability to make the costs of any Chinese invasion too high. By the late 1950s, and especially with fading Soviet support for Chinese irredentist claims, Beijing was forced to see the Taiwan problem as long-term. This shift of the issue to the back burner did not mean, however, that it ceased to be important.

This long-term strategy required a more subtle approach. It was certainly obvious that non-military means had to be tried. Obviously force of arms remained important, if only as a threat, but could not serve as a useful instrument for reunification. The more the sword was brandished, the further off the political target appeared. Thus the Sino-American *détente* of the 1970s opened up new possibilities for this peaceful long-term strategy.

China sought to isolate Taiwan politically, and starve it of military support. This meant a direct approach to the United States to cut its links to Taiwan. Thus China remained especially sensitive to American perceptions that Sino-American *détente* meant that Taiwan was no longer important. Far from it.

It was the Chinese view that Taiwan was as important as ever, but that its method for incorporation into the mainland was to be peaceful. This required the ending of United States arms sales and above all a growing sense in Taipei that it had no choice but to deal with Beijing. On both counts Chinese policy largely failed. Taiwan survives, and indeed flourishes as a pariah, but important trading partner for the West. The United States has reduced but not severed relations with Taiwan. The Taiwan problem has not gone away and remains the key symbol of China's unsatisfied national integrity. It therefore also remains the main problem for Sino-American relations. The main cosmetic deals have already been arranged, but the reality of an independent Taiwan remains as real as ever.

Taiwan and its associated islands are not the only unsolved territorial problem for China. The British and Portuguese colonies of Hong Kong and Macao have still not been reincorporated into China. But agreement with Britain in 1984 provided for the return of Hong Kong in 1997. This remarkable deal was the first time China has managed to peacefully negotiate the return of some sovereign territory. It was a triumph for Chinese diplomacy, in a sense regardless of the eventual fate of Hong Kong.

Yet the far more important reason for the long-term approach is related to the Taiwan question. Just as the Special Economic Zones (SEZs) are seen as examples of how China will manage the transition of capitalism into a socialist state, so Hong Kong is seen as an example to Taiwan of how its future will be managed. China is even offering Taiwan greater independence than presently promised to Hong Kong, but the example of Hong Kong's transition remains essential. In the end, China seems willing to sacrifice some economic gain in return for political principle and territorial integrity. The precise mix remains uncertain, but what is clear is that the military option is not ruled out.

China does have complete control, however, over how open it is to foreign influence. In the imperial past, before western attacks, China was largely closed to external influence. But the experience of the Qing dynasty, when the Chinese door was prised open by western traders, did not encourage many Chinese to believe that relations with the outside were good for China. An opposing view, perhaps more prominent in communist as opposed to nationalist China, emphasized that some positive foreign ideas, like Marxism, could be useful for China. However, the essential point is that China was ambivalent about opening itself up to the outside.

The emphasis on economic development, and compromise on allowing in some 'polluting' influences, is similar to that adopted in the Soviet Union over the past decades. It is also related to China's longer-term approach to the question of territorial integrity. The problems of China are now recognized for the difficult and intractable ones that they always have been. Thus the role of brute force and the military option is not stressed. The primary concern is now with long-term economic modernization. The new trend towards pragmatism and lower expectations in Chinese foreign policy is naturally derived from this longer term domestic strategy.

National Defence

Next to regaining Chinese territory, China's main foreign policy objective is to ensure its national defence. Chinese strategies in defence of its territory have often been peculiar, but the need is basic to almost every power. The special aspects of Chinese defence policy are essentially derived from the geographical situation.[8] China is not only the world's third largest state; it also has more neighbours than any other state. Thus, there is a basic threat derived from the multiplicity of defence problems, but also an opportunity provided for wide Chinese influence.

The human geography of China, at once the world's most populous country but also a poor peasant state, provides for strengths and weaknesses. Strength in that the population can support massive armed forces and produce a large GDP. Yet the weaknesses are more obvious; the most pressing is the need to feed more than one billion mouths daily and overcome the rural poverty of millions. China is clearly a great power, but it is also a poor power.

A more obvious defence dilemma has been the question of whether China should meet threats 'at the gates', or else sit back and allow an enemy to be swallowed in a sea of millions of hostile soldiers. Chinese defence policy has also been of two minds on whether to base defence on poor equipment but rich manpower resources, or else strive to modernize at least parts of the PLA. The bias, until recently, has been on 'man over weapons'.[9]

In forty years China has faced five major crises which raised these dilemmas. The Korean War (1950–3) showed China's willingness to take on a threatening power beyond China's borders. Despite the farce of Chinese 'volunteers', the PLA was engaged in lengthy combat in Korea. In fact, no subsequent PLA engagement was as costly as the Korean War. The PLA fought beyond the gates in defence of both China's national security, and in support of an allied communist regime.

The Korean War is instructive in various other important ways. First, it demonstrated China's willingness to run great risks in defence of an ally. To be sure, there were good reasons for China to fear for its own security, but the scale of the reaction indicates that some part of China's calculation was the need to support fraternal regimes. Second, China indicated a willingness to make sacrifices for allies, especially at a time of serious economic need in China itself. Third, the weaknesses of the PLA were shown up by the war. Despite becoming embroiled beyond its gates, the PLA proved to be a blunt instrument. Especially when confronting the modern United States armed forces, the strategy and arms of the PLA were deficient in many respects. Clearly the circumstances of the early 1950s did not allow China to act as confidently as it might have hoped. If the PLA could not succeed in the Korean War on China's borders, plainly it could not have an effective reach further afield.

China's next military engagement in defence of its national security did not come until nearly ten years later, and in the opposite corner of the country. The 1962 punitive war against India began with a Chinese perception of Indian territorial encroachments, and resulted in a Chinese strike into Indian territory.[10] The conclusions from this venture outside China's gates are different from the Korean case. Chinese success was also more clear than in Korea, but that was less due to PLA prowess, and more to the pathetic performance of the Indian army.

After the triumph of the PLA, Chinese defence policy acquired a new character in the area. India's long-standing quarrel with Pakistan helped bring China and Pakistan closer together. This tacit alliance developed despite Pakistani links with the United States. It was based overwhelmingly on the notion that 'the enemy of my enemy is my friend'. Chinese aid to Pakistan soon included military transfers and was encouraged during the 1960s by increasing Soviet–Indian alignment and the developing Sino-Soviet split. China thereby showed a willingness to act decisively to support its foreign policy, but even here there were limits.

In both the 1965 and 1971 Indo-Pakistani wars, China was

unable to offer any serious support to its ally in Pakistan. To be sure, there were diplomatic noises, but China was outgunned in threats of action by its Soviet neighbour that matched any Chinese signal with a more credible military threat. Thus Pakistan may have been China's ally, but China proved to be a paper ally in times of crisis. The circumstances that allowed China to defeat India in 1962 were special to the time, and did not mark any change in China's basic weakness in threatening military action in support of its foreign policy.

During the late 1960s, China faced its third defence policy problem. To the east the expanding United States presence in the Vietnam war raised the question of whether China should treat the threat as it had treated the threat in Korea. China made it plain to the United States that it would regard any crossing into North Vietnam as a threat to China. To that extent, Chinese deterrence extended beyond its gates, but was not tested.

However, Chinese deterrence was probed in a peculiar way by extensive United States bombing of North Vietnam. China became involved in the air defence of North Vietnam, firing on American aircraft and suffering casualties. This very mild form of defence beyond the gates, was in response to the controlled American threat to China's neighbour. Thus the parallels to the Korean War are close. China proved itself just as willing to engage the source of threat at an early stage and with serious military action.

However, there were important differences from the Korean experience. China's relations with Moscow were more strained in the 1960s, leading to a more independent Chinese military role. China's relations with North Vietnam were also less strong than in the Korean case. Vietnam was more able and willing to act on its own, while receiving aid from its communist allies. Thus China was less able to direct the combat, and the PLA was not called upon to become seriously involved. Thus the Vietnam war was not so much a test of PLA power, as it was of Chinese foreign policy resolve. It should be recalled that China did offer serious aid to Vietnam, and was not asked for more. The military seemed a useful, if limited instrument of Chinese foreign policy.

The fourth major threat to China's national defence is perhaps the most crucial, despite China having suffered the least amount of casualties in combat. The Sino-Soviet clashes of 1969 were in themselves fairly minor, although they were the most important fought by the Soviet Union since 1945. The true significance of these clashes lies in the potential threat they symbolize.[11]

The implications of the combat were felt far beyond the frozen ground on which they took place. China was eventually forced to the negotiating table by Soviet threats. Beijing realized that it had to take its northern neighbour seriously, especially in military terms. China and the Soviet Union were eventually to turn the struggle into a global competition to encircle each other.[12]

China responded with a combination of stratagems. Not only did it seek global support for its anti-Soviet campaign, China also concentrated on developing at least a minimal military capability that could raise the cost of a Soviet invasion. This deterrence by denial hinges not only on a threat to engage in a people's war, but also relies on a certain degree of military modernization. It is notable that there is little place for large-scale outside help in this modernization. For such basic aspects of defence, China must continue to rely on itself. Thus defence modernization remains a protracted process.[13]

China's weakness when facing the Soviet Union has not led it into entangling alliances. Despite tacit co-operation with the United States, China has no choice but essentially to rely on itself. Thus, when facing superior military power, China chose to take a low key position. When the Soviet Union invaded Afghanistan in December 1979, China expressed concern for a neighbouring state, but could offer no real resistance. China's ambivalence also ensued from Afghanistan being far from core China, and Afghanistan had already been conceded as a Soviet sphere of influence.

By the mid-1980s, because of China's clear priority on domestic economic development, Sino-Soviet detente began to ease tension on the Soviet front. The first moves towards Sino-Soviet *détente* were taken by China in the early 1980s. But when Mikhail Gorbachev came to power in 1985, it was the Soviet Union that sped up the pace. By May 1989, only a few months before China's fortieth birthday, China normalized relations with the Soviet Union and thereby completed the last major aspect of its foreign policy reform.

The Chinese no longer officially speak of a Soviet threat.

Tensions along the frontier have eased. The Soviet Union will have withdrawn close to 350,000 troops from Asia by 1990, thereby reducing its forces to nearly half the late 1970s' peak. China has already cut its armed forces by a million men and a further reduction of 500,000 was reportedly on the cards. The stage was set for formal arms control and confidence-building measures along the Sino-Soviet frontier.[14]

The final threat to Chinese national defence was less pressing than any of the previous four, but still resulted in massive Chinese casualties. The 1979 Chinese attack on Vietnam was an attempt to teach the Soviet Union that its allies could not run amok, especially in China's area of interest. On all counts, the use of Chinese force was unimpressive. While it is true that Vietnam did suffer massive damage in the north and was forced to make some adjustments to its troop deployments, in the end China lacked sufficient military clout to obtain its objectives.

In 1974, when China seized the Xisha islands from South Vietnam, Beijing showed that it could effectively use military force in the area. But the capture of those islands, claimed as Chinese territory, was achieved under special conditions. The enemy was the decrepit South Vietnamese regime, which was fighting North Vietnam. China's swift operation left little room for communist opposition to manifest itself against another communist state taking territory from the United States-supported South Vietnam.

In March 1988 China again took some islands from the Vietnamese in the South China Sea, this time in the Spratly group. In 1988 the enemy was Vietnamese communists, but the recipe for success was the same. Chinese success was both one of superior arms and excellent political timing. With growing Sino-Soviet *détente*, Moscow was unwilling to risk losing the bigger prize of improved relations with China, for the sake of keeping Vietnam happy.

In the 1979 war with Vietnam the two ingredients of past and future Chinese success were absent. Chinese action took place after Kampuchea was overrun by Vietnamese troops and left China with the more difficult military task of compelling rather than deterring Vietnamese action. What is worse, Vietnam had tacit Soviet support, thereby forcing China to wage a limited war against Vietnam that it could not win. The political objective of 'punishing' Vietnam hinged on a swift military success, and that was precisely what China could not achieve.

The implications of the 1979 war were in part similar to the previous cases. China showed a willingness to use arms to support its national defence, and also back up an ally in need. The use of the military instrument was beyond China's borders and entailed some serious sacrifice in men and material. However, in contrast to Korea, Chinese troops performed poorly. In Korea, they adequately defended North Korea, but in 1979 they failed to punish Vietnam. China's Kampuchean allies were relegated to a sideshow along the Thai frontier, and China was unable to help them break out.

China's poor showing in 1979 marked the low point in the effectiveness of the use of China's military instrument. The lessons learned were myriad, including the need for a less hostile view of Soviet power, and the need for thorough defence modernization. Most importantly, China perhaps saw that it was still a great power with not enough punch in the 'power'. The new sense of realism about what China could achieve in foreign policy in general was related to its realistic appreciation of China's military potential. The enduring dilemmas of Chinese defence policy remained. Uncertainty over defence beyond its borders, the question of the pace of military modernization, and the extent to which China needed to compromise with foreign threats, all were as difficult choices as ever. But as long as China remains essentially poor, and a great power with global concerns, these dilemmas will not disappear.

Economic Prosperity

As a continental economy, China has rarely sought economic prosperity by close contact with the outside world. In the past, curiosities were collected from as far afield as Africa, but the success of the Chinese state was defined and obtained back within core China.[15] Although China was ravaged by foreign powers for several hundred years before the communist revolution, modern China remained ambiguous about how much to open to the outside world for economic prosperity.

In the 1950s, prosperity and modernity were sought by forming an alliance with the Soviet Union and adopting the Soviet model. The impact of the Soviet Union on the Chinese economy is impossible to quantify. But given the desperate state of the Chinese economy at the time, even the limited assistance from the Soviet Union was vital for putting China back on its feet. The rapid Chinese growth had a great deal to do with simply taking up the slack of the past, but Soviet aid was vital to the speed and direction of modernization.

When China chose to pursue its own radical economic experiments, such as the Great Leap Forward in the late 1950s, no outsider could be held responsible for the failure. In fact, it was the Soviet Union that warned China that what it was doing was lunacy. The resulting death of some 25 million Chinese from famine was entirely China's fault, although it came at a time when China broke with the Soviet Union and Khrushchev withdrew his advisors in 1960. For close to 20 years, China then decided to go it alone in economic development. The result was the occasional spurt of success, followed by radical upheaval and economic failure. The Cultural Revolution was the primary example of the xenophobia and economic madness of domestic Chinese leaders.

With the death of Mao and the pursuit of Deng's reforms from 1978, China showed that it had learned its lesson. The decision to open China's door to the outside world resulted in a drastic increase in the percentage of Chinese GDP that was related to foreign trade.[16] Foreigners came to China in their millions as tourists and traders. Superficial changes, from advertising hoardings to snazzy hotels, showed just how serious China was about opening its doors. More importantly, foreign technology and expertise was bought in, not always successfully.

Most interestingly of all, China opened vast parts of its coastal territory for SEZs. The idea was to have certain parts of the economy drag the rest into the twenty-first century. The record was mixed, but there could be little doubt that China was serious about learning from the outside. This was the most sustained period of Chinese cosmopolitanism and it led to the opening of various open doors, including one to the north and the Soviet Union.

Of course, it is still too early to tell how successful this radical change in Chinese attitudes will be. China also sees the obvious benefits that come from playing a major role in international organizations. Basic features of the Chinese approach, including

racism to Africans or distance from any foreigner, remain characteristic of China's handling of the outside world. China is still
not happy about its open doors and they still swing and creak
on their hinges. But it is hard to see even a more nationalist
leadership closing China's doors to anything like the extent it
once did. In a more interdependent modern world, and one
that is even recognized as such nearly everywhere else in the
communist world, the idea of closing doors and ignoring the
global market economy seems unlikely and fruitless.

Global Influences

The fourth dimension of China's basic foreign policy concerns
takes it farther afield. The Chinese communists were interested
in far-flung international events well before they assumed power
in 1949. Even now, although lacking effective 'reach' in some
parts of the world, China sees it as necessary to have a fully
developed position. The motives for this desire for a global role
are several and often overlapping.

At the most basic level, as a large power with many borders,
China naturally extends further than any other power except
the superpowers. The Chinese very much see themselves as
'important', if only because one out of every four people in the
world is Chinese. What is more, China is a poor peasant state,
and unlike the superpowers, can claim to understand the developing world. China's efforts to lead the South against the North
are largely based on its self-image as the most important Third
World state.

China is not just a Third World state with Third World problems, it is also a state with a guiding ideology. The precepts of
that ideology are essentially universal, if only in urging world-
wide revolution towards socialism. The extent to which these
revolutionary objectives are pursued is, of course, a matter of
debate, even within China. At a time of major Chinese debate
about the meaning of their own ideology, it is hard for China
to argue that it has the correct answer for other developing
states. But the legitimacy of the CCP in China is based in part
on its ideology, and the ideology urges an international role. It
was precisely that ideology in the 1940s that gave the CCP a
global perspective of the place of the Chinese revolution.

Furthermore, the nature of the threats faced by China itself has involved it in international politics. China's major defence policy problems were to be found first with the United States, then the Soviet Union, and now with both together, which has led China to view its own foreign policy problems in global terms. Struggle against the United States and the Soviet Union involves other regions, in large part because the superpowers themselves see their role as international. Although China may know it lacks the long reach to compete with the superpowers in every distant crisis, China appreciates that what happens in those distant parts does affect China.

In the 1980s China even began to show that it had the reach of the superpowers. By supplying arms to both sides of the Gulf War, China was pursuing a pragmatic policy of making money. But it was also seeking some influence in that it hoped to have proven its friendship in time of need and also proven its ability to deliver goods on the scale and at the distance required by local states.[17]

Lastly, China has an acute sensitivity to what may happen if it ignores the outside world. The legacy of the imperialist's rape of China taught many Chinese leaders that they cannot ignore the outside world and close China's gates. In the end, a closed China is a weak China. Modern communications, and more effective military power deployed at a distance from the home base, make China potentially more vulnerable than in the nineteenth century. The solution to such weakness is seen in part by learning what is best from the outside, and creating alliances to deflect or reduce external threat.

This concern to avoid new international humiliation involves a basic desire to build up China's internal strength through modernization. But it also seems likely that this desire for a breathing space to develop internally will not result in a new isolationism if modernization should be achieved. Internationalism is not merely a tactic, it is a strategy for the continuing development of China.

Yet there remain serious challenges to internationalism as a guide to Chinese foreign policy. Certainly it defines much of China's longer historical practice. The Confucian and Sino-centric world view that dominated imperial China's view of the world has, of course, been overdrawn. But it remains true that China was relatively unbothered by the need for alliances or the complex international politics of Europe. While it seems clear that Chinese foreign policy in the twentieth century has broken away from these narrow ethnocentric perspectives, there remains an enduring Chinese perspective of cultural superiority. The jingoistic element has not been entirely absent from Chinese foreign policy in the past forty years.

Other motives for more Chinese isolation are derived from the economic backwardness of China. Some have argued that excessive concern with external relations only saps China's ability to deal with domestic problems. China lacks basic resources for a global foreign policy. While it might some day seek a more international role, in the short term it must concentrate on its own affairs. In a country as poor as China, these arguments can be persuasive.

On balance, there remains a basic dilemma. Does China seek global influence, or does it concentrate more on domestic problems? This is not merely a matter of ideology versus pragmatism, for there are ideological justifications for both isolationism and internationalism, for both a closed and open door. The dilemma remains unresolved, and China has experienced various different ways of coping with the choices.

In the first phase, after Korea and during the Sino-Soviet honeymoon, China sought as many friends as possible. The drive for international recognition derived from various sources, including a desire to overcome the legacy of pre-revolutionary humiliation, and the need to win friends in order to isolate Taiwan. This brought China into direct confrontation with United States power, but China chose not to confront the threat directly. The Bandung phase of the five principles of peaceful coexistence was best served by a low-key emphasis on Chinese demands, and more enhanced by a broad smile and professions of friendship.

This phase had some obvious success. China was not seeking direct aid, or pushing the revolutionary cause very firmly. The minimal desires were therefore more easily satisfied, especially by other Third World states seeking friends in a hostile and polarized cold war world. China did support some revolutionary movements, but they were mostly close to home, and relatively uncontroversial as the opponents were western-supported regimes. China certainly lacked any long reach into distant parts of the Third World and so, wisely minimized this aspect of its ideological objectives. Thus, it is not surprising that China's gains in this period were swift and relatively easy. China established a reputation in the Third World as sympathetic, if less useful than the Soviet Union. However, the honeymoon did not last long.

The developing Sino-Soviet split in the late 1950s and the early 1960s brought out the sharper side of Chinese policy. The basic drive was still internationalist, but more radical and assertive. China now had to justify its position not only against the 'imperialist' West, but also against the communist Soviet Union. The relatively simple desire for revolutionary change became clouded when China urged 'true' revolution and not the moderate Soviet version. China seemed more concerned with confronting Soviet-supported causes than in challenging western-dominated movements. Most importantly, China's splitting of the revolutionary cause upset many of its former friends in the Third World. While they may have agreed with China's long-term objectives, and felt China was more sympathetic to their problems, they were concerned that Beijing was undermining revolutionary unity. What is more, China lacked the economic clout to support its radical posture, and so left the Third World states and movements with the choice of support from China in words, or arms and aid from Moscow.

It is therefore not surprising that Chinese policy suffered. The campaign for recognition was slowed as some states came to see China as the more revolutionary wing of the communist movement. States that supported India and Yugoslavia in their moderate leadership of the non-aligned were disconcerted at China's 1962 war with India and the sharp attacks on Tito in the struggle with the Soviet Union. This Chinese policy was still internationalist, but it was a more radical variant that led to more isolation than global influence. From the mid-1960s the trend became more rather than less radical.

In fact, the Cultural Revolution was a time of a virtually non-existent foreign policy. All ambassadors but one were recalled to China, although this did not mean that China ceased to pay any attention to the outside world. But while China had a position on most international issues, it was invariably a radical one that did not last far into the 1970s. But when China returned to an active foreign policy after the double shock of the Soviet invasion of Czechoslovakia and the Ussuri river clashes, it found the world less sympathetic.

During the 1970s, as Chinese foreign policy shifted to a perception of the Soviet Union as the main threat, Beijing was disconcerted to find the going somewhat tough. The reasons were essentially fourfold. First, after the radical excesses of the Cultural Revolution, China was no longer seen as stable. The purge of Lin Biao and the factional politics of radicals and moderates in the 1970s enhanced this image. Secondly, the failure of the Cultural Revolution took the shine off China's revolutionary appeal. The evident inability of Chinese leaders to cope with the problems of making revolution in a Third World state did not attract those who sought a coherent model for revolution. Thirdly, China still lacked the economic and military power to support these revolutionaries. If China was now seen as being as much of a revolutionary failure as the Soviet Union, then it was best to take aid from the Soviet Union who could at least offer far more material assistance than poor China. Fourthly, China's new sharp anti-Soviet foreign policy often upset many Third World states and movements. Unlike the 1960s when China at least opposed both superpowers equally, in the 1970s it was an often uncomfortable associate of the United States simply because it was at the time taking an anti-Soviet position. Support for conservative regimes in Zaire, or Chile, did much damage to China's image.

The latest phase of Chinese policy began about 1980 with a series of internal and external policy reassessments. The foreign policy changes towards greater pragmatism and openness had essentially three dimensions. First, Chinese leaders recognized the failure of many of their past domestic experiments. The judgement on the role of Mao Zedong meant that China could begin to chart a new future. It meant a policy of retaining certain 'Maoist' elements, but also far greater pragmatism in adopting new, and even foreign ideas. This was then a major motive for a return to a more internationalist perceptive, but also one that sought to learn as much as to teach others. It was a return to the Bandung phase, but with less grandiose dreams, and with less basic need to obtain recognition. Unfortunately, the problems were more protracted ones of developing influence, and developing China's own economy.

Secondly, China abandoned its one-sided anti-Sovietism in favour of a more balanced challenge to both superpowers. This is not to suggest that China saw both superpowers as equal, and in collusion and contention as in the 1960s. This time, China saw some issues in which the United States' policy was the primary problem, for example, Central America and the Middle East. It also saw other issues, such as Southeast Asia or Afghanistan where the Soviet Union was the major problem. The great advantage of this new dual-adversary posture was that it afforded China far more flexibility. China abandoned any pretence of an overarching theory of international politics, such as the much discredited Theory of Three Worlds. In its place, China offered merely vague support for the South in its claims against the North, and urged all states to abide by the Five Principles of Peaceful Coexistence. China's main focus of attention seemed to be in establishing itself as the champion of the South against the North.

Yet China's new concern with the Third World did not go hand in hand with a massive aid programme. Unlike previous phases of involvement in Third World politics, China now recognized more openly the limits to its power. It pleaded poverty like most Third World states, and drew on international monetary arrangements as did many other members of the South. To be sure, some Chinese aid programmes were evident, but the scale was much reduced. What is more, Chinese relations with many Third World states, especially in the OPEC subcategory of the Third World, involved more normal economic deals and trade that benefited China's own domestic development projects.

China still sees the Third World as important. The old motive of seeking international recognition is no longer present. But the desire to win friends and influence is still relevant. China's renewed concern with international politics focuses on threats posed by both superpowers, and China does see that it can play a role in helping the Third World throw off superpower pressures. Yet China is also far more pragmatic and long term in its approach than in previous decades. The problems of international divisions in the Third World are now more openly acknowledged by China. Beijing's own limitations in providing aid are also recognized, but unlike in the past, China does not try to make grandiose promises or offer confident advice in lieu of real aid.

Directions of Change

Has Chinese foreign policy been a success in the past forty years? The answer in 1989 must be positive, although the Chinese clearly took a circuitous route to their ends. They have fought more major wars than any other great power since 1949 and they certainly have lost more men in combat. They now stand with a bit more territory than when they began. Apart from Tibet, there have been tiny territorial gains in the offshore islands, the South China Sea and the border with India. Hong Kong and Macao will return in a decade's time. Apart from the South China Sea region, there is little prospect of any further Chinese gains.

China is a more prosperous place than it was in 1949, in part because it has learned from the outside. But there have been great lost times and opportunities. China left most of its doors closed for so long, that it is remarkable that they have done quite as well as they have in the past forty years. Comparisons with the NICs of East Asia, and especially Taiwan, suggest just how much more China could have done and needs to do in the future.

In broader terms, China's global influence has less clearly improved. In the West, China is now seen as a pleasant, but still poor place that is of marginal importance to their prosperity or power. The dreams of the China market have mostly faded, as have images of China as NATO's 16th member. Sino-Soviet *détente* in the late 1980s makes the West even more wary.

The communist world is warier still of China. Although relations are better now than at any point since the 1950s, the high point was earlier in the 1950s. Most of the developing world sees China in less friendly terms, with the possible exception of the Middle East. China has few real friends in Asia and tension with ASEAN states may well increase as the sense of a Soviet and Vietnamese threat fades. Despite the increased number of diplomatic relations, and despite the slogan about 'having friends all over the world', China has fewer real friends than at previous points in the past forty years.

Yet it might be most fair to judge Chinese foreign policy in terms of Chinese perceptions rather than those of foreigners. From the Chinese perspective, they are more prosperous and more at peace than at any time in the past forty years. Although it did not need to take forty years to get to where China is now, at least it has managed its limited successes. Only the most churlish would not be thankful for small mercies.

1. Gerald Segal and William Tow, *Chinese Defence Policy* (London: Macmillan, 1984), and Gerald Segal, *Defending China* (Oxford: Oxford University Press, 1985).
2. Michael Yahuda, *China's Role in World Affairs* (London: Croom Helm, 1978), and *China's Foreign Policy After Mao* (London: Macmillan, 1983).
3. A. Doak Barnett, *The Making of Chinese Foreign Policy* (Boulder: Westview, 1985).
4. Paul Godwin, *China's Defence Establishment* (Boulder: Westview, 1983).
5. Lucian Pye, *The Dynamics of Chinese Politics* (Cambridge: Oelschager, Gunn and Hain, 1981).
6. Yahuda, *China's Foreign Policy*.
7. Allen Whiting, *China Crosses the Yalu* (N.Y.: Macmillan, 1960), and *China's Calculus of Deterrence* (Ann Arbor: University of Michigan Press, 1975).
8. Segal, *Defending China*.
9. Ellis Joffe, *The Chinese Army After Mao* (London: Weidenfeld, 1987).
10. Whiting, *China's Calculus*, and Neville Maxwell, *India's China War* (London: Jonathan Cape, 1970).
11. Richard Wich, *Sino-Soviet Crisis Politics* (Cambridge: Harvard University Press, 1980).
12. Gerald Segal, *Sino-Soviet Relations After Mao* (London: IISS, Adelphi Paper No. 202, 1985).
13. Joffe, *Chinese Army*.
14. Gerald Segal, ed., *Arms Control in Asia* (London: Macmillan, 1987), and 'Sino-Soviet relations: The New Agenda', in *The World Today*, June 1988.
15. S. A. M. Adshead, *China: A History* (London: Macmillan, 1988).
16. Martin Lockett, 'The Economy', in David Goodman, Martin Lockett, Gerald Segal, *The China Challenge* (London: Routledge for the RIIA, Chatham House Papers, 1986).
17. Anne Gilks and Gerald Segal, *China and the Arms Trade* (London: Croom Helm, 1985).

8. Taiwan and the Reunification of China

LEE LAI TO

IN recent years, social and economic contacts between the People's Republic of China and the Republic of China on Taiwan via third countries have become commonplace. Peace in the Taiwan Straits has also been maintained and it is not likely that the status quo will be disturbed in the near future. However, when coming to the knotty issue of the reunification of China, it seems that all the proposals from the Chinese Communist Party (CCP) government on the mainland have been rebuffed by the Kuomintang (KMT) government in Taiwan. In turn, Taipei seems to be mapping out a new 'counter-offensive' confident that it will be able to prevail over the other side eventually. This article examines the proposals from the post-Mao leaders in Beijing, and the reasons for Taipei's reactions. It will also consider the KMT's strategy on reunification in the light of Taiwan's domestic developments and international relations. Finally, the paper will cast an eye on the future of relations between the two sides of the Taiwan Straits.

Beijing's Initiatives

While the post-Mao leaders of China have clearly been preoccupied with the four modernizations, Beijing has also made efforts to bring Taiwan into its fold. To achieve what it considers to be its historical mission to unite China, Deng Xiaoping had in mind to 'strive for the actualization of including Taiwan in the unification of the motherland' in the 1980s.[1] This was demonstrated by various proposals for that purpose from leading CCP figures like Deng Xiaoping, Ye Jianying, Deng Yingchao, Liao Chengzhi, Zhao Ziyang and Hu Yaobang.[2] As the Sino-British negotiations on the future of Hong Kong began to bear fruit, it became clear that the master plan of the post-Mao leaders for reunification would be the 'one country, two systems' formula. Much publicity and elaboration have been given to this in China. In a nutshell, what this proposal amounts to is the incorporation of Taiwan into China as a Special Administrative Region (SAR). The Taiwan SAR would maintain its socio-economic system, armed forces and economic and cultural ties with other countries. China promises not to interfere with the local affairs of Taiwan, its way of life and the judiciary. Preparatory legislation was enacted by inserting Article 31 into the Chinese constitution providing for the establishment of an SAR when necessary. Apparently, this will be applied to Hong Kong, Macau and eventually Taiwan. All three have been promised a high degree of autonomy. The major difference for Taiwan lies in the promise that it could keep its own armed forces.

At the 13th Party Congress, Zhao Ziyang officially propounded, among other things, what is called 'the primary stage of socialism in China'. According to him, China is only at the beginning of its socialist road, and it will be at least one hundred years from the 1950s before socialist modernization is accomplished. In the meantime, China must emphasize modernization, reform, open policy and develop diverse sectors of the economy with public ownership playing a dominant role in the primary stage.[3] In other words, public ownership, while dominant, will be accompanied by individual or private ownership, Sino-foreign joint ventures, Sino-foreign co-operative enterprises and wholly foreign-owned ventures in the primary stage to boost productivity. This new theory in many ways further supports the 'one country, two systems' proposal in the sense that it legalizes and enhances the acceptability of the SARs where capitalism is practised under more autonomous conditions in a socialist state.

In view of the vast differences between China and Taiwan, the logic of the Beijing leaders in having 'one country, two systems' is to preserve socialist superiority on the mainland but maintain prosperity in 'capitalist' Taiwan. The latter could also be used to beef up the economy of socialist China. However, the CCP has not disguised the fact that, under such a formula, Taiwan will be a local government and that only a unitary, not a federal, not to say a confederal government, will be acceptable. By extension, such a structure will be governed by what the CCP calls 'the four cardinal principles', namely, 'upholding the socialist road, the people's democratic dictatorship, leadership by the Party and Marxism-Leninism and Mao Zedong thought'.

In proposing the adoption of 'one country, two systems', Beijing has opted for a grand design that could hopefully solve the reunification issue. Because of their lack of experience in incorporating capitalist enclaves, it would like to experiment with the formula in Hong Kong first. However, it seems that ageing leaders in China would like to see Taiwan reunited with the mainland in their lifetime. Before the death of Chiang Ching-kuo in January 1988, the old guard in China reminded their counterparts, especially Chiang Ching-kuo, that they should try to solve their differences so that history would be kinder to them. Their awareness of a sense of history and their place in it no doubt has contributed to China's reiteration of having three exchanges: exchange of mail, trade, and air and shipping services. The hope is to build up the momentum to expedite the process of reunification. Beijing has also proposed a third united front between the KMT and the CCP. This did not cut much ice and is actually a misreading of the thinking of many of the KMT old guard in Taiwan. As many know, the KMT's experience in co-operating with the CCP in the two united fronts, one from 1924–27, the other from 1937–45, was bitter and the two united fronts ended in bloodshed.

To the leaders in Beijing, Taiwan, Hong Kong and Macau are problems left over by history, although they are also aware of the fact that Taiwan is a much more difficult nut to crack as the latter is a *de facto* independent state having a relatively well-to-do populace. China's seeming hurry, however, is not without its rationale. Notably, it worries about the rise of an independent Taiwan and has threatened to use force in such an eventuality. As elaborated later on, the Taiwanization in the pre- and especially post-Chiang Ching-kuo KMT government, the dilution of familial ties across the Taiwan Straits, the fight for independence inside and outside Taiwan all pave the way for a Taiwan that is less attached to the mainland. Certainly, the socio-economic not to say ideological gulf may be reinforced, if not widened, if Taiwan develops in its own way for longer periods.

To entice Taiwan to the conference table to talk about reunification, Beijing reiterates the political and economic benefits that would result from co-operation between the CCP and the KMT. It argues that reunification is inevitable and conforms with Chinese nationalism and patriotism. Behind all these peaceful initiatives, Beijing also tries to exert pressure on Taipei directly or indirectly. While it cannot do much about domestic developments in Taiwan, Beijing has been quite successful in isolating Taiwan diplomatically. Its insistence that there is only one China and that the PRC is the representative of China has been widely accepted. This has forced Taiwan to resort to other unconventional methods to keep in touch with the world, and to a certain extent has made it difficult for Taipei to operate in world affairs.[4] However, it is also clear that Beijing is willing to tolerate the existence of unofficial or semi-official relations between Taipei and other countries. In addition, Beijing would not really object to the existence of Taipei in international organizations provided the latter takes part under names such as 'Taipei, China' or 'Chinese Taipei'. This conforms with Beijing's policy of relegating Taiwan to a local or secondary position in China. It would also probably allow more exchanges, though not necessarily pleasant ones, between the two sides in such forums. It would also soften the blow against Taipei diplomatically. It should be noted that, in principle, Beijing has always insisted that the Taiwan problem is an internal affair which brooks no interference from other countries. In actual practice, it has asked other countries, at least in the case of the United States, to exert its influence on Taiwan to establish more contacts with the mainland.[5] While many countries would be more than reluctant to get involved in the quagmire of the China–Taiwan conflict, it seems that Beijing is not totally unreceptive to the role of a third party if the latter is in a position to serve as a messenger or better still a mediator between the two sides of the Taiwan Straits.

Taipei's Response and Strategy

To Beijing's various proposals for reunification the standard answer from Taipei has been negative and it proposes instead reunifying China under Sun Yat-sen's 'Three Principles of the People'. Officially, the request to have 'three exchanges' by

Beijing has been met with Taipei's 'three-noes' policy: no contact, no compromise and no negotiation. Such a response gives
the impression that Taipei has been evasive and that it is not
really interested in reunification, at least for the time being.
Taipei's seeming rigidity in its approach should, however, not
disguise the fact that it has become relatively more flexible. This
has been demonstrated in various ways such as the participation
of Taiwan in international athletic competitions under the name
of 'Chinese Taipei'; negotiations between China Airlines (CAL)
and Civil Aviation Administration of China (CAAC) officials
for the return of a hijacked CAL plane to Taipei; and the decision
to stay in the Asian Development Bank even though its name
has been changed to 'Taipei, China'. On top of these, there are
people-to-people contacts, and trade between the two sides
through third countries.[6]

More dramatic steps were taken during the last few months
of Chiang Ching-kuo's regime in Taiwan. Related to the reunification issue was Taipei's announcement that it would relax the
ban on importing Chinese publications which did not promote
communism. Taiwan also dropped its ban on direct travel to
Hong Kong and Macau. Most important of all, family visits
to the mainland via third countries have been allowed since
November 1987. Although the KMT still maintains that there is
no change in its 'three-noes' policy and that family visits to the
mainland are allowed for humanitarian reasons, it is obvious
that in the last months of his life, Chiang Ching-kuo must have
thought of changing Taiwan's policy towards the mainland.

Chiang seemed to have come to the conclusion that the reunification of China under the Three Principles of the People would
have to be supplemented, if not modified, by other more concrete measures. In view of the rapid socio-economic changes
and the evolving desire to have a more open and democratic
society as a result of the transformation of Taiwan from a developing into a newly industrializing economy, steps would have
to be taken to cope with these trends. At the end of his life,
Chiang probably thought that it was no longer realistic to expect
the KMT to replace the communist regime on the mainland. His
major concern would be the preservation of the KMT regime in
Taiwan. As he surveyed the situation on the island, he, just like
his adversaries on the mainland, would be concerned with the

fact that certain segments of the population had advocated the independence or 'self-determination' of Taiwan. With the passage of time, both mainlanders and Taiwanese would have a more nebulous identification with the mainland, making it plausible for the independence movement to gain momentum.

The lifting of the ban on family visits to the mainland could be construed as one of the first moves to rekindle the ties between the two sides before they drifted too far apart. More important, it is a way to dilute the influence of the independence movement and consolidate or perpetuate KMT rule on Taiwan. The lifting of the ban was a belated recognition of the fact that an estimated 10,000 Taiwan people were already visiting China annually via third countries. Moreover, the tide of visits to the mainland by people from Taiwan was surging. For one thing, many of the mainlanders and old soldiers who followed the KMT to Taiwan were homesick. They wished to visit their home towns and the mainland before they died. Chiang Ching-kuo probably did not want to be remembered as someone who was responsible for the separation of Taiwan from the mainland.

As the influence of the Chiang family was being diluted and since Chiang Ching-kuo had said that Taiwan after him would not be headed by any member of the Chiang family, it was possible that Chiang Ching-kuo took the initial steps to link the two sides of the Taiwan Straits so that history would be kinder to China under the Chiangs when judging the reunification issue. Obviously, if Taiwan's mainland policy were ever to change it would be easier under Chiang, in view of his dominance in the politics of the island.

No doubt there was opposition to the new moves towards the mainland. However, Chiang's stature proved to be most useful in overcoming these obstacles. And to be sure, the so-called liberals were supporting Chiang. Notably, the reform-minded Secretary-General Lee Huan tried to tone down the rhetoric about 'recovering' China under the banner of the Three Principles of the People. Instead, Lee remarked in September 1987 that the KMT did not intend to replace the communists on the mainland. According to him, the strategy henceforth was to launch 'a political offensive' to demand the democratization of politics, freedom of the press and the liberalization of the economy on the mainland.[7]

This no doubt reflected a realistic assessment of the ability of the KMT and the place of the CCP on the mainland. It was probably clear to Lee Huan and others that it was not likely that the KMT would be able to recapture the mainland. With enhanced confidence as a result of Taipei's remarkable economic performance and plans to liberalize the polity and economy, the 'reformers' intended to compete with the mainland by demonstrating the success of the 'Taiwan model'. As such, renewed contacts with the mainland by allowing family visits was just one step in this direction as the Chinese on both sides of the Taiwan Straits could then find out for themselves which side had done better since 1949.

After the death of Chiang Ching-kuo in January 1988, and the emergence of Lee Teng-hui as his successor as president of Taiwan and acting chairman of the KMT, there was renewed pressure for a more liberal policy towards the mainland. More practical arguments were presented to change the mainland policy. Notably, some businessmen in Taiwan wanted to branch out into China. The rise of protectionism in the West, including Taiwan's major trade partner, the United States, has forced the business community to look for alternatives. Taiwan's huge trade surplus in its trade with the United States has not only strained Taipei–Washington relations, but added more pressure on Taiwan to increase the value of the Taiwan dollar, open its market to the outside world and decrease its exports to the United States. To be sure, the Taiwan dollar has been appreciating, adding more pressure to Taiwan's export industries. In addition, increasing labour costs, lack of natural resources and surplus capital have forced businessmen in Taiwan to look for new trade and investment opportunities. China in the midst of a drive to modernize offered such opportunities but the Taipei government imposed restrictions. No doubt, businessmen could conduct trade and investment through third countries like Hong Kong; but this method always runs the risk of incurring the wrath of the Taipei government. Thus the hope was that trade with and investment in the mainland, especially through third countries, would be condoned officially later on.

Apparently, the 'China fever' that emerged after the lifting of the travel ban in November 1987 created high expectations for a major change in Taiwan's mainland policy at the 13th KMT

Congress in July 1988. The euphoria was vividly demonstrated by the fact that by July 1988, more than 100,000 had made family visits to the mainland since the travel ban was lifted.[8] There were also many discussions in the mass media and academic community on problems related to Taipei–Beijing relations, a phenomenon unprecedented in the history of Taiwan. As it turns out, the KMT opted for incremental change in its policy towards the mainland at the 13th party congress. Notably, the KMT congress decided to broaden its contacts with the mainland by condoning investments in China via third countries. It legalized two-way trade with China through Hong Kong and other third countries and officially approved a list of commodities that Taiwan may import directly from China. Policy guidelines on visits between the two sides of the Taiwan Straits also seemed to have been relaxed considerably. Among these was the disclosure that Taiwan would review requests from mainland Chinese to visit Taiwan for funerals or in cases where immediate relatives were seriously ill. Intellectuals who 'denounce Marxism-Leninism or who have fought to maintain academic freedom' might also be allowed to visit Taiwan. These measures broaden the categories of mainland Chinese permitted to enter Taiwan. Previously, all were barred from entering Taiwan under the National Security Law unless they were at least 75 years old or under 16 and had relatives in Taiwan, or unless they had lived as a permanent resident in a 'free country or area' for at least five years. For the people of Taiwan, the KMT announced that it would study the possibility of allowing participation by its athletes in international competition on the mainland and consider allowing its journalists to go there on reporting assignments.[9] Other guidelines from the congress included permission to import academic, technological, literary and artistic publications from the mainland after screening. Copyright of mainland authors would also be protected.

Although the KMT congress reiterated the 'three-noes' policy, it is obvious that it has been modified, if not changed, by the new guidelines. However, it is significant that the KMT ruled out official links or direct trade with China. It should also be pointed out that the major concern of the KMT was not, and is not, the reunification issue. From the deliberations of the 13th Congress it appears that the KMT was obviously more concerned with the internal problems of the party and Taiwan. The rejuvenation of the central committee, the triumph of the reform-minded in the congress, and the higher proportion of native Taiwanese in the new KMT central standing committee indicate that the KMT needs time to heal internal political wounds. Party organization and discipline will probably be emphasized to strengthen the KMT and to meet future challenges.

The KMT also intends to introduce a programme of political and social reforms through the government, as revealed at the congress. These include the registration of civic organizations and political parties; retirement for a large number of the members of the Legislative Yuan, Control Yuan and National Assembly representing constituencies on the mainland; and giving Taiwan provincial government and its assembly more autonomy. The KMT's preoccupation was the consolidation and perpetuation of its rule in Taiwan. Any changes in its mainland policy were relegated to secondary importance and have to be examined in the light of that preoccupation. Besides, the KMT is always afraid that the united front tactics of the CCP will gobble Taiwan up and it cannot but be conscious of the fact that the CCP has not renounced the use of force in its reunification policy. As the lifting of the ban to visit China was introduced recently, the KMT would need more time to monitor the situation to determine if it was necessary to expedite the pace of change in its policy towards the mainland.

Any fundamental change in the KMT's mainland policy would most likely change its 'three-noes' policy. A premature gesture in linking up directly with the mainland might arouse the suspicion of the anti-communists and give the excuse to the 'successionists' in Taiwan to act drastically. In addition, the new team under Lee Teng-hui does not really have the same political clout, connections and influence as Chiang Ching-kuo in expediting the tempo or pace of reunification at this point. They still need time to build up their support and influence. As such, they could ill-afford, even if they wanted, to fundamentally change Taiwan's mainland policy for fear of creating dissent and division within Taiwan.

It was clear that the KMT felt more relaxed in allowing people from Taiwan to visit the mainland through indirect channels and that this would not be prohibited. Apparently, the KMT concluded that such visits did not present any security problems to Taiwan.[10] Moreover, such visits would enhance the appreciation of the people in Taiwan of what they have under the KMT government and increase the knowledge of the 'Taiwan model' on the mainland. Similarly, permission to allow mainlanders to come selectively to Taiwan would improve Taiwan's image. On the economic front, the KMT still treads a very cautious line. Notably, direct investments and trade with the other side remain prohibited. The prime reason could be that Taipei does not want to be overly dependent on China. In fact, the Taipei government, while condoning indirect investments and trade warns its business community of the risks involved in relying too much on the China market. At a time when Taipei wants to upgrade its industries and to increase its technological know-how, it probably also finds it less desirable to allow its businessmen to venture into various labour-intensive projects on the mainland. This may slow down its industrial upgrading and render Taipei less competitive in the international economy. Moreover, it is argued that direct trade would give the wrong signals—that Taiwan is moving towards unification prematurely—and consequently produce the kind of problems discussed earlier.

The Road Ahead

As the 1980s draw to a close, it seems that the CCP will not be able to reunify China in the near future. While it has welcomed visitors and investments from Taiwan with open arms, it is also concerned about recent domestic developments within both the KMT and Taiwan. With a majority of Taiwanese on the Central Standing Committee of the KMT headed by a Taiwanese, Lee Teng-hui, and the inevitable trend of Taiwanization within the party and government, Beijing quite naturally will have more worries about the desire for independence on Taiwan. In the future, it not only has to deal with a more Taiwanized KMT and government, but an emerging opposition, especially the Democratic Progressive Party, thus complicating the road to reunification. No doubt Lee Teng-hui is still following the line basically laid down by his mentor Chiang Ching-kuo. He has, for example, toned down the anachronistic slogan of 'recovering' China under the Three Principles of the People. His party and government are now easing restrictions on indirect contacts. However, direct mail, flight, shipping, trade and investments between the two sides remains prohibited. More important, except for some low-level or unauthorized official contacts between the two sides, the KMT has been refusing to hold talks with the other side officially. It has rejected the concept of 'one country, two systems' and even those who are more inclined to work for reunification in Taiwan find the proposal unpalatable.

In the future, Beijing will have to deal with the 'political offensive' launched by the KMT and its promotion of the 'Taiwan model' alongside the furtherance of democratic and economic reform on the mainland. Apparently, Beijing has not considered this a threat and in the case of social visits and trade, it probably believes that there are more advantages than disadvantages in continuing and promoting such endeavours. Quite obviously, Taiwan enjoys a higher standard of living and this will reflect negatively on China. However, Beijing may believe that the appeal to emotions will some day bring Taiwan back to the fold. These contacts may also promote a better and more realistic understanding of each other's problems. The CCP is surely confident enough that it has established itself domestically and internationally, and that Taiwan could not be a threat to the mainland. From Beijing's perspective, it would be ideal were Taiwan, or for that matter, Hong Kong, to be incorporated into China. The resources in those areas certainly could be tapped to upgrade development on the mainland. While it is difficult for the mainland to catch up with the two newly industrializing economies, it would not be difficult for certain parts of China, especially the big cities and SEZs to narrow the gap in the future. China's political and economic reforms and the evolution of what is called in China, 'socialism with Chinese characteristics', may also make it easier in time for Taiwan to consider reunification.

It remains to be said that in the near future China will continue to harp on the theme of having 'one country, two systems' for reunification. Its most important step in this direction will certainly be the implementation of such a formula in Hong Kong, as this will set an example for both Taiwan and Macau. Thus the drafting of the Basic Law and the successful incorporation of Hong Kong as an SAR in 1997 will be the most important items on the CCP's agenda. Care must be taken to make the principle of 'one country, two systems' as practised in Hong Kong more appealing to Taiwan, without at the same time compromising the right of the CCP to interfere should developments endanger its interests. The CCP also has to decide whether the KMT and its representatives should stay in Hong Kong after 1997. From all indications, it seems that the CCP would not object to some kind of KMT presence in Hong Kong. Hong Kong is and will be used until 1997 as a contact point between the two sides of the Taiwan Straits. Even after 1997 Hong Kong can be useful to Beijing in performing the same role provided the KMT does not contemplate destabilizing the situation in the SAR.

Since the KMT has rejected the 'one country, two systems' proposal, the CCP needs to think of some other measures to promote reunification. With its concern for modernization and retention of the open policy, China seems to be in a more tolerant and pragmatic mood to talk about reunification. It will be interesting to see if China is willing to refrain from the use of force and amend its constitution to accommodate the interests of the KMT in Taiwan after an initial period of contacts and a review of the situation in the Taiwan Straits.[11]

On the Taipei side incremental changes in its mainland policy are primarily a product of domestic developments. Since it cannot stem the tide of people from Taiwan going to China for trade, investment and social visits, it may well make the best use of the situation. It is pragmatic enough to fine-tune its policy to a level that could help it politically and economically. As far as reunification is concerned, it is trying its best to slow the move in that direction so that it could strengthen its bargaining position before meeting its counterpart at the conference table. Economic prosperity, 'democratization' and localization of the polity will not only strengthen the KMT's hold on Taiwan, but also outdistance the performance of the CCP on the mainland, at least in the near future, thus making it more difficult for the CCP to blur the differences between the two sides of the Straits. Notably, the further co-option of Taiwanese and the *de facto* and eventually *de jure* recognition of the place of the opposition could be used by the KMT to strengthen its anti-communist stand and demand similarly 'democratic' developments on the mainland before reunification. As travel between the two is basically one-sided—from Taiwan to the mainland—the KMT is in a better position to exploit the situation on the mainland.

With regard to Hong Kong, the initial KMT response to the Sino-British agreement of 1984 was that all links with Hong Kong would have to be cut by 1997. However, there was subsequently a pragmatic recognition that it would wait and see how things develop in the colony. It seems that after a careful reassessment, the KMT decided that its 'official' organizations will stay in Hong Kong until at least 1997.[12] The KMT has probably concluded that it would be difficult to replace Hong Kong's role completely because of the latter's geographical proximity to the mainland and the wide range of networks and connections with China. For practical reasons, Hong Kong will, at least in the near future, continue to serve Taiwan and other countries as an attractive place to establish a base for the China market. Even after 1997, it seems that the KMT would like to retain some kind of presence in Hong Kong, if possible, again primarily for trade and investment purposes.[13] Although it does not accept the 'one country, two systems' proposal, it could monitor the application of the formula and exert whatever influence it might have on the 'democratic forces' in the SAR. Just in case its presence in Hong Kong after 1997 becomes less welcome, Taiwan may try to look for alternative bases in Tokyo or Singapore. If it can, it would also like to take over Hong Kong's role as a financial centre and attract some of its resources.

Beijing would clearly like to establish Hong Kong as an example of the successful application of the 'one country, two systems' formula. At the same time Hong Kong could certainly serve some practical purposes for Taiwan before and after 1997. Consequently, it seems that Hong Kong will remain as an important contact point for the CCP and KMT. As far as the KMT is concerned, it has probably concluded that it has more to gain in having a stable Hong Kong in the future. It goes without saying that the KMT will try to maintain its contacts with China in Hong Kong unofficially, at least in the near future. However, it has yet to decide if it should have direct contacts with the Hong Kong SAR, once that comes into existence, or think of some other ways to establish indirect contacts with Hong Kong.

Since Taiwan is isolated in the international community and has diplomatic relations with only twenty-two states, it will attempt to use economic diplomacy to win friendship with other countries. It will make use of its economic power to demonstrate to the outside world—through unofficial or semi-official channels—that Taiwan has done well.

It may also entice others to have closer economic and even political co-operation with Taipei. The hope is that these third parties will be more sympathetic towards Taipei or at least neutral in the China–Taiwan conflict in the sense that they will not exert undue pressure on Taipei to negotiate with the mainland when coming to the issue of reunification. This is especially true in the case of the United States which could have considerable influence on the reunification issue *if* it wants to.[14] From all indications, it seems that Taipei will also fight its way back in some international organizations, especially those of a socio-economic nature. It seems that the KMT has recognized that it is unwise to walk out of an international organization whenever China is present as this will give China the floor and isolate Taiwan further in the world. It is quite clear that the long-time policy of rejecting dual membership with China in international organizations is changing. With its new-found confidence and affluence, Taiwan's insistence on retaining its official name, the Republic of China, in some instances has been toned down and it has become and will be pragmatic enough to create some other means of participation in international affairs.

At present and also for the near future, various formulae or models of reunification are largely irrelevant as conditions in both China and Taiwan are not yet far enough advanced. Taiwan has no interest in talks with China on reunification, and it thinks that its domestic and international situation is not favourable to negotiations with Beijing. While China is keen to plunge into talks on reunification, it lags far behind Taiwan in economic development and there is a wide gap between the two sides in political and socio-economic terms. It will take quite some time for China to narrow the gap to make Taiwan more receptive to its reunification overtures. In view of these, it is premature to map out grand designs or models for reunification and it is more productive to concentrate on confidence-building gestures to lay the foundations for eventual official talks in the future. As such, the emphasis in the future should be on more pragmatic and mutually beneficial measures such as the promotion of a realistic understanding of each other and trade. While the Chinese on both sides of the Taiwan Straits may want to have one China and some may console themselves by saying philosophically that *fen jiu bi he* (unity must come after a long separation), the road towards reunification will be long and tortuous.

1. Deng Xiaoping, *Jianshe You Zhongguo Tese De Shehui Zhuyi* (Building Socialism with Special Chinese Characteristics), revised edition, (Hong Kong: Joint Publishing Co., 1987), p. 3.
2. For an analysis of these proposals, see Lee Lai To, 'The PRC and Taiwan—Moving Towards a More Realistic Relationship', in Robert Scalapino *et al.*, *Regional and Global Security Issues in the Pacific-Asian Region* (Berkeley: Institute of East Asian Studies, forthcoming).
3. *Beijing Review*, 9–15 November, 1987, Documents, pp. III–XI.
4. Lee Lai To, op. cit.
5. Chen Qimao, 'The Taiwan Issue and Sino-U.S. Relations', *Asian Survey*, November 1987, p. 1175.
6. *Far Eastern Economic Review*, 1 October, 1987, p. 30.
7. Li Da, (ed.), *Kaifang Taiwan* (The Opening of Taiwan) (Hong Kong: Wide Angle Press, 1988), p. 36.
8. *The Free China Journal*, 18 July, 1988, p. 12.
9. Ibid.
10. *The Free China Journal*, 1 August, 1988, p. 2.
11. At the time of writing, it was reported that some senior Chinese officials have made known to James Hsiung, a political scientist teaching in the United States that China is willing to discuss the drawing up of a new constitution to accommodate the interests of the KMT. It is also reported that China is prepared to remove the use of force if Taiwan agrees that it should revert to China. Whether this will become the official policy of China remains to be seen. See *Far Eastern Economic Review*, 1 September, 1988, p. 26.
12. *The Nineties* (Hong Kong), April 1988, pp. 42–4.
13. Li Da, (ed.) op. cit., pp. 116–23.
14. Officially, the United States does not want to play the role of a mediator in the China–Taiwan conflict. It also does not want to put more pressure on Taiwan to consider the reunification gestures from China and re-open the China issue in its domestic politics. For details, see Lee Lai To, op. cit.

9. Hong Kong and China: Economic Interdependence

MICHÈLE LEDÍC

ECONOMIC relations between China and Hong Kong are complex, close and longstanding, and in recent years have become more intense. Is this just a result of China's open door policy or a combination of that and other factors? How will relations develop after 1997, and how far will they affect trade between the United Kingdom on the one hand and China and Hong Kong on the other. This article considers some answers to these questions. It begins with a comparison of the size and nature of the two economies as they are now, and examines how important they are to each. Secondly, it examines visible trade flows between China and Hong Kong, including the role of intra-trade, and the growing importance of outward processing activities.

The flow of capital, in the form of direct investment by China in Hong Kong, as well as Hong Kong investment in China, particularly in the Special Economic Zones (SEZs), is an even stronger indicator of interaction between the two economies. The growth of these relations since 1979, and especially since 1984, when the Sino-British Joint Declaration on Hong Kong was signed, is also discussed. In considering future economic relations between Hong Kong and China, the article first analyses the current position and then assesses whether the year 1997 is likely to represent a dramatic change or just a continuation of present trends. Finally, it briefly assesses the implications of all these developments for United Kingdom trade.

The Economies of China and Hong Kong

To compare the economies of China and Hong Kong is, from many points of view, an exercise that makes little sense. How can one compare a huge country such as China, in terms of population, resources and area, with a tiny one such as Hong Kong? Bearing in mind these differences, and also those between

Table 1 *Comparison of Income Levels*

	GDP US$ bn		AAR (%) GDP	AAR (%) GNP per capita	GNP per capita
	1965	1985	1965–85	1965–85	US$ 1985
China	65.59	265.53	7.2	4.8	310
Hong Kong	2.15	30.73	14.2	6.1	6,230

Source: *World Bank Development Report, 1987.*

the role of government in the two economies, it is nevertheless of interest to compare their rates of growth in the recent past, and their present living standards. In addition, it is important to examine the structure of their economies: this is not because one expects the structure to be similar, but because one is interested in how far the two economies complement each other at present, and how they might be expected to do so in the future, as their economic relationship becomes closer. The comparisons that follow are made with these considerations in mind.

Hong Kong's Gross Domestic Product (GDP) in 1965 was some 3 per cent of China's GDP. Twenty years later it was nearly 12 per cent. China's GDP during this period had an average annual growth rate of 7.2 per cent, while Hong Kong had nearly double this rate of growth, both measured in constant US dollars (see Table 1). However, measured in Hong Kong dollars, on a real basis, Hong Kong's GDP growth rate has been only a little over 8 per cent per annum, while China's average growth rate of national income, measured in Chinese yuan, has been around 8.6 per cent.

In the same period, GNP per capita in China grew by 4.8 per cent per annum and in Hong Kong by 6.1 per cent. In 1985 China's GNP per capita was US$ 310, while Hong Kong's was twenty times higher, at US$ 6,230.

The two economies differ greatly in the composition of their output, especially in the importance of agriculture and services. Both of these sectors had slower growth rates in China over the last twenty years than the industry sector.

The composition of Hong Kong's GDP is much more like that of an advanced country, with a very low proportion of output coming from agriculture, a high proportion from services, and

Table 2 *Composition of GDP in 1985 (percentage)*

	Agriculture	Industry	Services
China	45	47	8
Hong Kong	1	31	68

Source: *Statistical Yearbook of China 1987*; Hong Kong, 1987.

with the service sector expanding much faster than the rest of the economy.

The links between China and Hong Kong are very strong. Between 1979 and 1987 Hong Kong's trade with China increased, in current prices, by over ten times, and since 1985 China has been Hong Kong's largest trading partner.

At the same time, Hong Kong is China's largest export market, with some 35 per cent of China's total exports going to Hong Kong in 1987. Hong Kong is China's largest source of direct foreign investment and joint venture investment. It is an *entrepôt* of great importance for China's exports, most recently regarding trade with South Korea and Taiwan. It is estimated that 30 to 40 per cent of China's foreign exchange receipts are earned through Hong Kong.[1] Remittances sent from Hong Kong to relatives in China are a valuable source of income for China.

Chinese investments in Hong Kong are large and growing. They have overtaken British investments in the manufacturing sector, and are now exceeded only by American and Japanese. Chinese interests control 15 banks in Hong Kong, and numerous other companies.

Foreign Trade of China and Hong Kong

Exports are of growing importance for China, increasing from 7.4 per cent of national income in 1980 to about 14 per cent in 1987. These figures compare with 13.8 per cent for Japan, 22.1 per cent for the UK, and 88.7 per cent for Hong Kong in 1984, and a very high figure of 108 per cent of GDP for Hong Kong in 1987.[2]

There has recently been a substantial change in the composition of China's trade, and its exports in particular. Manufactured goods in 1985 accounted for 43.9 per cent and in 1987

158 *Michèle Ledíc*

Table 3 *China: Commodity Composition of Trade*

	1985 (%)	1986 (%)	1987 (%)	% change in value 1986/85	% change in value 1987/86
EXPORTS	100.0	100.0	100.0	+33.8	+35.6
Primary goods	50.7	36.4	33.7	−4.2	+26.0
Manufactured	49.3	63.6	66.3	+72.6	+40.3
IMPORTS	100.0	100.0	100.0	+19.1	+11.8
Primary goods	12.4	13.1	16.0	+25.7	+43.3
Manufactured	87.6	86.9	84.0	+18.2	+7.1

Source: *China's Customs Statistics No. 1*, 1986; *No. 1*, 1987; *No. 1*, 1988.

for 66.3 per cent of total exports. Their value, in current prices, increased to nearly 2.5 times the 1985 level.

Exports of primary goods, which include oil, declined by some 4 per cent (in current prices) between 1985 and 1986, but overall exports increased by nearly 34 per cent. Many observers predicted a sharp decline in export performance in 1986, due to the oil price collapse, especially as China's oil and oil product exports earned 22.3 per cent of total foreign exchange in 1985. Crude oil and oil product exports were halved to some US$ 3.8 billion in 1986, in comparison with the year before, while in volume terms they were only 6.3% lower. The same trend continued into 1987. Petroleum and petroleum products accounted for only 10.1 per cent, while textiles and clothing (with a value of US$ 9.55 billion) for 24 per cent of total export earnings.[3]

Few countries could have emerged from the 1986 oil crisis with such a quick and effective response, with China switching its exports from mainly primary to manufactured goods, notably to textiles and clothing. Textiles and clothing exports grew by 53 per cent and 46 per cent respectively in 1986 and 1987. Combined with import controls, this enabled the trade deficit to be reduced from nearly US$ 15 billion in 1985, to US$ 3.7 billion in 1987.[4]

Import controls, following an explosion of manufactured goods imports in 1985, accounted for the fact that manufactured goods imports increased less, both in 1986 and 1987, than imports of primary products (see Table 3).

Hong Kong and Japan were the most important partners in

Table 4 *China's Top Five Trading Partners in 1987*

	US$ billion	% in total imports	% change 1987/86
EXPORTS			
Hong Kong and Macao	14.2	36	+50
Japan	6.4	16	+44
United States	3.0	8	+24
West Germany	1.2	3	+29
Soviet Union	1.2	3	+9
(United Kingdom	0.5	1	−60)
Total of above	26.5	67	
Total	39.5	100	+35
	US$ billion	% in total imports	% change 1987/86
IMPORTS			
Japan	10.1	23	−13
Hong Kong and Macao	8.6	20	+60
United States	4.8	11	+11
West Germany	3.1	7	−7
Soviet Union	1.3	3	−7
(United Kingdom	0.9	2	−5)
Total of above	28.8	66	
Total	43.2	100	+11

Source: *China's Customs Statistics No. 1*, 1988.

China's foreign trade in 1987. Together they accounted for 52 per cent of its exports and 43 per cent of its imports. However, in bilateral terms the trends were very different. China's imports from Japan fell by 13 per cent (after a 17 per cent decline between 1985 and 1986), while exports increased by 44 per cent, as compared with 1986. Trade with Hong Kong took a different direction, with imports and exports both increasing by 60 per cent and 50 per cent respectively.

Hong Kong's trade in the last couple of years has been growing very fast indeed, and China's share in it has become substantial. In 1987, 31 per cent of Hong Kong's imports and 46 per cent of Hong Kong's re-exports came from China, while 14 per cent of Hong Kong's domestic exports went there. Some 33 per cent of total Hong Kong's re-exports were destined for China. Re-exports accounted for nearly 70 per cent of all Hong Kong exports to China.

Table 5 *Hong Kong Trade and China Dimension (All values in HK$)*

	1985		1986		1987		Change 1987/85
	$bn	(%)	$bn	(%)	$bn	(%)	(%)
IMPORTS	231.4		275.9		377.9		+63
China	58.9	(25)	81.6	(30)	117.3	(31)	+99
DOMESTIC EXPORTS	129.9		154.0		195.2		+50
China	15.2	(12)	18.0	(12)	27.9	(14)	+83
RE-EXPORTS (destination)	105.3		122.5		182.7		+73
China	46.0	(44)	40.9	(33)	60.2	(33)	+31
TOTAL EXPORTS	235.2		276.5		378.0		+61
China	61.2	(26)	58.9	(21)	88.0	(23)	+44
RE-EXPORTS/TOTAL EXPORTS		(45)		(44)		(48)	
China		(75)		(69)		(68)	
Memo Item:							
RE-EXPORTS OF CHINA's GOODS	34.6	(33)	51.6	(42)	84.3	(46)	+143

Source: Hong Kong 1987; Hong Kong 1988; Hong Kong External Trade, December 1987.

Trade figures that are not shown separately in Chinese statistics, but are given in detail for Hong Kong, are those of re-exports. Two types of re-exports are differentiated: re-exports of goods to China from the rest of the world, by country of origin, and goods imported from China, and re-exported to the rest of the world. In addition, some imported Chinese goods are processed in Hong Kong and re-exported to China.

Hong Kong's total re-exports in 1987 amounted to HK$ 182.7 billion. HK$ 60.2 billion of these re-exports went to China, and HK$ 84.3 billion came from China. China was therefore involved in Hong Kong re-exports, amounting to HK$ 144.5 billion, or nearly 80 per cent of the total, either as a market or as a source of supply. Total Hong Kong re-exports to all countries increased in value terms more than 70 per cent between 1985 and 1987. Re-exports are of growing importance in the total exports of Hong Kong: in 1985 they accounted for 45 per cent of total exports, rising to 48 per cent in 1987.

China's share in Hong Kong's total re-exports from the rest of the world has varied in the last three years between 33 per cent and 44 per cent. A great swing occurred in 1985 with a huge increase in China's imports compared with 1984. Hong Kong's re-exports to China increased by some 65 per cent to reach a value of HK$ 46 billion (US$ 5.89 billion). With the introduction of more stringent import controls in China in 1986, they fell to HK$ 41 billion. However, with import controls still in operation in China in 1987, Hong Kong's re-exports in value terms increased by 50 per cent over 1986, to reach HK$ 60 billion. Since China's total imports only went up by 11 per cent this means that Hong Kong (whose domestic exports to China rose by 50 per cent also) is taking a larger share of imports than previously. These flows of re-exports from Hong Kong show that Hong Kong's role as an *entrepôt* for China is increasing in importance year by year. This surge in business may be partly due to Hong Kong's role as an *entrepôt* in the booming indirect trade of China with Taiwan and South Korea. China's total trade with Taiwan and South Korea (via Hong Kong) amounted to an estimated US$ 1.5 billion (up 57 per cent) and US$ 1.2 billion (up 87 per cent) respectively in 1987.[5]

The second type of re-exports that the statistics recognize are those of goods imported from China and re-exported to the rest of the world, China included. Re-exports of Chinese goods have been increasing steadily, and between 1985 and 1987 rose by more than 140 per cent in value terms. The share of this type of re-export in total re-exports from Hong Kong has risen from 33 per cent in 1985 to 46 per cent in 1987 (see Table 5).

Much of the mutual growth in trade over the last couple of years can be explained by increased outward processing activities in China, on behalf of firms in Hong Kong. Large-scale outward processing is a relatively new phenomenon, dating back to 1984, and is now in full swing. An increasing number of simple but labour-intensive production processes, previously carried out in Hong Kong, have been moved to the nearby Guangdong province, to take advantage of lower production costs, especially those of labour.

Most of the products are assembled in China and then sent back to Hong Kong as finished goods, or as semi-finished goods needing further processing, possibly qualifying thereby for Hong Kong origin (particularly important in the United States market). Products for which the qualifying manufacturing processes are carried out in China would be regarded as of Chinese origin. Even when goods from China are subject to value-added manufacturing processes in Hong Kong, they may not qualify for Hong Kong origin, and would be regarded as a re-export from China.

In addition to the majority, who are using the cheap labour in order to manufacture for export, some Hong Kong manufacturers have set up factories in China in the hope of gaining easier access to China's domestic market. Some estimates quote a figure of 10,000 factories in Guangdong province, either processing for Hong Kong companies or in co-operative ventures with them, and employing no less than 1 million workers. Hong Kong's manufacturing labour force is now just over 1 million, so that it could be argued that Hong Kong's effective labour force has in fact been doubled as a result of co-operation with China.[6] The commodity composition of trade between the two countries has been much affected by outward processing. Most Hong Kong toy and electronics manufacturers, and a large number of textile and garment companies, have their manufacturing carried out in Guangdong.

Textiles and garments are the dominant categories in trade between the two countries. Overall trade statistics for Hong Kong reveal that in 1987 24 per cent of Hong Kong's exports to China, and 28 per cent of re-exports, were of textiles and clothing. In the same year, 41 per cent of Hong Kong's imports of these items were from China.

The value of Hong Kong's exports and re-exports of textiles and clothing to China in 1987 amounted in 1987 to HK$ 21.6 billion and its imports to HK$ 48.0 billion, both increasing by nearly 40 per cent over 1986.[7] What is happening is that yarns from Hong Kong are being made into fabrics in China, and either exported in this form, or made into clothing and exported. Similarly, fabrics from Hong Kong are being made into clothing for export from China to Hong Kong. In addition, China has long been a principal source of fabrics and clothing for Hong Kong. Most of the clothing is used for Hong Kong's own needs, but the fabrics are processed further in Hong Kong, making possible a significant proportion of Hong Kong's clothing exports.

Hong Kong's third most important export and re-export item to China (miscellaneous manufactured articles are second) is telecommunications equipment, amounting to HK$ 8.1 billion in all (an increase of 55 per cent over 1986). Imports of this category from China were HK$ 7.1 billion (an increase of nearly 80 per cent over 1986). The relative size of these figures suggests that this item included some 'true' exports and re-exports from Hong Kong to China as well as outward processing on the part of Hong Kong.[8]

Investment in China and Hong Kong

Apart from trade, two-way investment constitutes an important part of the economic relationship between China and Hong Kong. Available data on foreign investment in China show that between 1979 and September 1987 foreign investment contracted was in the region of US$ 23.7 billion. Of this, nearly US$ 15.5 billion or 65 per cent came from Hong Kong and Macau. In the SEZs Hong Kong's share was nearer 80 per cent. Japan was responsible for about 12 per cent and the United States 10 per cent of total contracted foreign investment during the same period.[9]

It is well known that realized foreign investment in China is much below the contracted figure. It has been estimated that only one-third of contracted investment has in fact been realized. Because of the problems involved, concerning, for example, legislation and the repatriation of foreign exchange—as well as ever-changing parameters as, for example, the cost of power, labour, and taxes—contracted investment has been falling. China contracted foreign investment of US$ 3.3 billion and US$ 3.7 billion in 1986 and 1987 respectively, which represented a substantial fall from the figure of US$ 6.3 billion in 1985. Contracted foreign investment, in the form of equity joint ventures, has been mainly in property and hotels (48.5 per cent), light industry, including textiles and clothing (20 per cent), and machinery and appliances (17.5 per cent). Energy and resources, with 10 per cent, and all others, with only 4 per cent, were not very attractive for contracted foreign investment. Total realized foreign investment in China was US$ 1.96 billion in 1985, and rose to US$ 2.24 billion in 1987.[10]

Much of Hong Kong's investment in the SEZs has been connected with the desire to create facilities to enable outward processing to take place. A large number of industrial co-operation projects have been concluded between Hong Kong and China. Many have not involved substantial investment in fixed assets, but have used the existing labour force and local industrial premises, and have provided some plant and machinery, as well as training. According to the Hong Kong Industry Department, a total of 216 industrial co-operation agreements were made with China in the fourth quarter of 1986. Of these, 193 projects, or 89 per cent, involved subcontracting arrangements and outward processing. They related mainly to the plastics, electronics, textiles and clothing industries.[11]

Apart from investment in China's industrial and services sectors, Hong Kong capital is also involved in the development of infrastructure in China. Two Hong Kong firms signed a letter of intent to set up a joint venture power plant in Jiangsu in 1987. More important, the Daya Bay nuclear power plant project is a joint venture between the Hong Kong Nuclear Investment Company and the Guangdong Nuclear Investment Company.

In addition to direct investment, substantial loans have been extended to China from Hong Kong. In 1985 loans totalled HK$ 3 billion (US$ 385 million), some 50 per cent more than in the previous year. In addition, short-term commercial loans in 1985 were estimated at about HK$ 3.9 billion (US$ 500 million).[12] In the same year China borrowed overseas a total of some US$ 2.5 billion (an increase of nearly 95 per cent over 1984), of which Hong Kong provided more than 20 per cent of the total. According to the Ministry of Foreign Economic Relations and Trade (MOFERT) China borrowed US$ 5 billion in 1986, double the 1985 and quadruple the 1984 amount.[13]

Flows of foreign investment into Hong Kong have a very different pattern. Overall foreign investment in Hong Kong's service sectors, particularly banking and finance, has always been very strong, but foreign investment in Hong Kong's manufacturing industries has accounted in the past for a relatively small proportion of the private sector share of gross domestic fixed capital formation. However, statistical data on inward investment in the manufacturing sector, in respect of projects facilitated by the Industry Department, show a sharp rise since 1984.

Recently, two areas have been identified as a key to confidence in the future of Hong Kong's economy: investment in Hong Kong and capital outflows from Hong Kong. A serious lack of confidence in the future of Hong Kong's economy would be quite

Table 6 *Investment in Hong Kong's Manu-facturing (current prices)*

	Value of inward investment HK$ million	US$ million
1983	12	1.54
1984	40	5.13
1985	286	36.67
1986	500	64.10

Source: *1986 Survey of Overseas Investment in Hong Kong's Manufacturing Industry.*

inconsistent with the trend of inward investment shown in Table 6. It is true that there has been a net capital outflow, but much of the outflow can probably be explained by higher interest rates in the United States than in Hong Kong for considerable periods in recent years.

Further evidence of confidence in the future of Hong Kong's economy is to be found in Hong Kong's own private sector investment in plant and machinery. Despite a small decline in investment in plant and machinery in 1985 (there was then strong growth in 1986 that continued into 1987) Hong Kong has enjoyed the highest ever average annual investment in plant and machinery during the four-year period 1984 to 1987. Over the same period, retained imports of industrial machinery for use in the manufacturing sector grew by 15 per cent per annum in real terms. In the first half of 1987 retained imports of capital goods grew by 25 per cent, and imports of machinery for use in the manufacturing sector by 20 per cent.[14]

Another financial phenomenon gaining momentum in Hong Kong is Japanese investment, not only in financial services, but also in the manufacturing sector. It has been estimated that to March 1980 Japan's direct foreign investment in Hong Kong was of a cumulative value of US$ 1 billion. Since then a large increase to nearly three times this level has been reported. For example, Japan in 1986 invested some US$ 2.3 billion in Asia, of which 22 per cent went to Hong Kong (US$ 506 million). The combination of Japanese technology and capital, Hong Kong capital, and low-cost Chinese labour, provide the seeds of a new, self-reinforcing relationship of mutual interdependence in east Asia.[15]

Most Chinese investment in Hong Kong is relatively recent (although there has been some long-standing investment, for example, by the Bank of China group). Between 1980 and 1984 China invested some US$ 5–6 billion in a number of fields, including trade, transportation, construction, real estate, manufacturing and financial services. Chinese investors generally preferred to buy existing companies, thus gaining the expertise that came with them.

A survey carried out by the Hong Kong Industry Department in 1986, covering the manufacturing sector, showed that China had become the third largest foreign investor, with 18.4 per cent of the total capital, following the United States (36.4 per cent) and Japan (21.1 per cent). Britain ranked third in a survey carried out in 1984, but had fallen to fourth place in 1986. Chinese investment concentrated mainly on non-metallic mineral products, electronics (except toys, watches and clocks), printing and publishing, textiles and clothing and chemical products. In 1986, of 33 establishments acquired, employing more than 5,000 workers, 9 were wholly owned by China and 26 were joint ventures. It is reported that some 2,000 companies in Hong Kong now have Chinese backing.[16]

Chinese interests control 15 banks in Hong Kong and numerous other companies as well. A Chinese company bought 15 per cent in Cathay Pacific Airways in 1987, and China is participating in a consortium that is building a second cross-harbour tunnel. There is no doubt that China is now engaged actively in building up its stake in Hong Kong's economy.

Future Economic Relations Between Hong Kong and China

The Sino-British Joint Declaration, which was ratified in 1985, guarantees the continuation of Hong Kong's present rights and freedoms for a period of fifty years after 1997. Hong Kong will retain its capitalist system, its freely convertible currency, its status as a free port and its own customs territory. It will conduct its own economic and cultural relations, and continue to participate in international organizations. This gives investors the assurance that their rights will be protected, and that their profits can be freely converted into foreign currencies.

Will the Joint Declaration operate in practice? This is the

question that is asked by all businessmen in Hong Kong, and by all present and potential foreign investors there. Britain and China have had continuous discussions on implementation since 1985, especially in the Sino-British Joint Liaison Group. Agreement has been reached in a number of important areas, notably trade, travel and communications. For example, Hong Kong became a member of GATT in its own right in 1986, has begun to conclude its own air service agreements, and to set up its own shipping register. All this has been provided for in the Draft Basic Law—a 'mini' constitution for Hong Kong. This was published early in 1988 and is still under discussion. Its most controversial economic provisions are that it contains a legal requirement that Hong Kong should have a balanced budget and a low tax policy after 1997. There have been many objections to this. In fact these provisions are a matter of current Hong Kong government policy, but it is argued that there is no place in a constitution for requirements of this kind.[17]

Hong Kong has enjoyed high economic growth in the last two years, in spite of the major stock market crash in October 1987. The average annual growth of the GDP in real terms was 12.5 per cent. Helped by the fall in the exchange value of the United States dollar, to which the Hong Kong dollar is linked, domestic exports grew by 23 per cent at current prices in 1987 (inflation was 6 per cent) and re-exports by 46 per cent. As we have seen, foreign investment in Hong Kong has been at a high level, and includes substantial investment from Japan.

There is no sign in all this that there are strong international doubts about the future of Hong Kong's economy. In particular, China's growing investment in Hong Kong suggests that it looks upon Hong Kong as a separate economic entity for the foreseeable future. It wants a share of Hong Kong's prosperity, and finds it valuable to have a stake in an economy on which it is dependent for an estimated 30 per cent to 40 per cent of its total foreign exchange receipts.

The strong development of intra-trade between China and Hong Kong has taken place to a considerable extent as a result of China's open door policy, but confidence in the future of Hong Kong must have played a part on the Hong Kong side. If this had not been the case, it seems unlikely that Hong Kong investors and entrepreneurs would have invested in China to

Table 7 *United Kingdom Trade with China and Hong Kong (£ million)*

	1982	1986	1987	change (%) 1987/86	1987/82
EXPORTS					
China	103	536	416	−22.4	+303.9
Hong Kong	732	961	1,013	+5.4	+38.4
IMPORTS					
China	193	327	391	+19.6	+102.6
Hong Kong	873	1,530	1,531	+0.06	+75.4
TRADE BALANCE					
China	−90	+209	+25		
Hong Kong	−141	−569	−518		

Source: *Overseas Trade Statistics of the UK*, 1985; 1986; 1987.

the extent that they have, or would have made co-operative agreements on such a large scale.

In these circumstances, it seems unlikely that 1997 will be of great economic significance for either China or Hong Kong. The two economies are likely to have grown closer together by then. The effects of the Joint Declaration will already have been taken into account, and no great change is likely to take place in 1997, or afterwards, other things being equal. The events of May and June 1989 in China are likely to have an effect on this scenario. It is however too early to foresee the full, long-term consequences for Hong Kong and China, and the relationship between them.

The United Kingdom Dimension

The United Kingdom has had a trade deficit with Hong Kong for a number of years. In 1987, for example, United Kingdom exports to Hong Kong amounted to £1,013 million and its imports to £1,531 million, an export/import ratio of 66 per cent. However, re-exports are included in the figures. Since Hong Kong re-exports more to the United Kingdom than it imports from the United Kingdom for re-export to other countries, the United Kingdom's apparent trade deficit with Hong Kong is exaggerated.

Until recently, the United Kingdom had a deficit with China

also, but since 1984 it has had a surplus, according to the United Kingdom data. In 1987 United Kingdom exports to China were £416 million and imports £391 million, an export/import ratio of 127 per cent. Hong Kong has grown in importance as a bridge between the United Kingdom and China, with about 10 per cent of United Kingdom exports to China, and 14 per cent of United Kingdom imports from China, going through Hong Kong.

United Kingdom figures show increased imports from China in 1987. But according to Chinese statistics almost all of China's leading trade partners bought more from China in 1987 than they did in 1986 (see Table 4), with the exception of the United Kingdom, which purchased 60 per cent less and sold 5 per cent less, keeping the balance in its favour. Chinese statistics contradict the United Kingdom figures for 1986 as well. Customs figures show a 370 per cent surge in British purchases from China, resulting in the United Kingdom's being one of the few industrialized nations with which China had a surplus in that year.

The United Kingdom share of Hong Kong's imports has fallen from 5 per cent in 1979 to 3.1 per cent in 1987, and its share of imports of manufactured goods from 6.2 per cent to 3.7 per cent over the same period. Imports into Hong Kong of manufactured goods from China increased greatly over these years, however, and it is not therefore surprising that the United Kingdom share in manufactured goods should have shown a substantial fall.

The United Kingdom's share of Hong Kong imports of manufactured goods from the main industrial suppliers (Japan, the United States, the United Kingdom, West Germany, Italy, France and Canada) fell between 1981 and 1986 from 10.7 per cent to 8.8 per cent. Nevertheless, the United Kingdom's share of the Hong Kong market is the same as its share of the world market, while Germany, France and Italy have achieved only about one-third of their world average performance. It has been concluded by the Hong Kong Government Office, London, that, on a relative basis, United Kingdom exports do three times as well as those of Germany, France and Italy in Hong Kong.[18]

In China, on the other hand, the relative position is reversed. In recent years direct United Kingdom exports to China compare unfavourably with those of Germany and Italy. The United Kingdom does well, however, in re-exporting to China through

Hong Kong, as compared with her main European rivals. The conclusion seems to be that the United Kingdom is successful in Hong Kong, but less so when exporting direct to China from the United Kingdom. Britain therefore benefits when using Hong Kong as an intermediary or partner.

Will anything change as a result of the approach of 1997, other things being equal? This depends on how far trade and investment between the United Kingdom and Hong Kong have in recent years depended on political links which will formally end in 1997. This is a question that is not easy to answer, but here again it may well be the case that the Joint Declaration has already been taken into account. Economic relations between Hong Kong and the United Kingdom, and between China and the United Kingdom, may soon become similar therefore to those that apply at present between Hong Kong and China on the one hand and the other major industrial powers on the other. The United Kingdom will, in future, have no alternative but to compete with its international rivals on an equal basis in China and Hong Kong.

1. See 'Hong Kong Works', talk given by Mr. K. Y. Yeung, the Director of Industry, Hong Kong Government, at a seminar held in London on 7 September 1987. Also 'Hong Kong in Transition', speech given by Sir David Wilson, Governor of Hong Kong, at Chatham House, London, on 21 March 1988.
2. Source: 1986 Almanac of China's Foreign Economic Relations and Trade (Hong Kong, 1986), p. 924; Hong Kong 1988 (Hong Kong Government Information Service, Hong Kong, 1988).
3. Michèle Ledíc, 'The Energy Sector', in David S. G. Goodman (ed.), *China's Regional Development*, London: Routledge, 1989), p. 105; *China's Customs Statistics*, No. 1, 1988 (General Administration of Customs of the People's Republic of China, Hong Kong, 1988), Table 4.
4. *Xinhua*, 14 January 1988, in SWB FE/W0010 A/9, of 27 January 1988.
5. Source: Hong Kong Government, see also: *Business China*, Vol. XIV, No. 17, September 1988, p. 132.
6. David Dodwell, 'A Boom Made in China', *The Financial Times*, 11 September 1987.
7. Hong Kong External Trade, December 1988 (Hong Kong, 1988).
8. Ibid.
9. *Guoji Shangbao* (International Business), 30 January 1986, p.1; *Far Eastern Economic Review*, 19 March 1987; *Xinhua*, 21 March 1988, in SWB FE/W 0020 A/8 of 6 April 1988.
10. Source: Ministry of Foreign Economic Relations and Trade (MOFERT), see also: *The Financial Times*, 29 September 1986; State Statistical Bureau Communiqué of 23 February 1988; *The Economist*, 12 November 1988, p. 84.
11. 1986 Survey of Overseas Investment in Hong Kong Manufacturing Industry (Hong Kong Industry Department, Hong Kong, 1987).

12. *The Economist*, 27 August 1988, pp. 65–6.
13. *Far Eastern Economic Review*, 26 March 1987, p. 53 and p. 80.
14. Hong Kong 1988, op. cit., p. 55.
15. *The Economist*, 12 September 1987, p. 12; *Far Eastern Economic Review*, 7 April 1988, pp. 49–86.
16. 1986 Survey of Overseas Investment in Hong Kong, op. cit.; see also: Masaki Furuhashi, 'The Movement of Chinese Capital into Hong Kong', *China's Newsletter, JETRO*, No. 62, 1987, pp. 4–11; 'The Role of Hong Kong', speech by Mr. Selwyn Alleyne, Hong Kong Commissioner in London, at the CBI Conference, London, 3 October 1988, p. 4.
17. For further analysis of the Draft Basic Law and related issues see: Sino-British Joint Declaration on the Future of Hong Kong (HMSO, London, 1984); The Draft Basic Law of the Hong Kong Special Administrative Region of the People's Republic of China (Hong Kong, April 1988 and February 1989); 'Hong Kong '88', *Far Eastern Economic Review*, 7 April 1988, pp. 49–86; Joseph Y. S. Cheng, 'Hong Kong: The Pressure to Converge', *International Affairs*, Vol. 63, No. 2, 1987, pp. 271–83; William McGurn (ed.), *Basic Law, Basic Questions* (Hong Kong: Review Publishing Co. Ltd., 1988); Michèle Ledíc, 'Hong Kong's Economy under the Draft Basic Law', paper presented at SOAS seminar on the Draft Basic Law for Hong Kong, London, June 1988; *The Hong Kong Law Journal*, Vol. 18, No. 3, 1988, pp. 421–5.
18. Adam Baillie, 'Waiting for T-Day', CBI News, 21 November 1986, pp. 30–57; Briefing Papers, Hong Kong Government Office, London, August 1987.

INDEX

Index compiled by Peva Keane